MORE THAN MERE SURVIVAL

More Than Mere Survival

Conversations with Women Over 65

Jane Seskin

NEWSWEEK BOOKS, New York

Printed in the United States of America

Library of Congress Cataloging in Publication Data

Seskin, Jane.
More than mere survival.
Bibliography: p.
1. Aged women—United States—Biography. 2. Old
age. I. Title.
HQ1064.U5S47   305.4   79-3549
ISBN 0-88225-288-7

Book design: Mary Ann Joulwan

CONTENTS

Thanks are due:

To the women who allowed me to share their homes and offices, their opinions and ideas. They patiently answered my questions with honesty, they extended their hands in friendship. I owe them a part of my future.

To women friends who have stood the test of time: Corinne Ageloff, Linda Breslau, Ilene Cooper, Carolyn Goudsmit, Ronnie Greenberg, Janet Harris, Patricia Hinkley, Margo Husin, Marsha Kaminsky, Marcia Pollak, Mary Triest Ross, Ellen Schmalholz, Nancy Shapiro, Susan Shapiro, Joan Solomon, Joan Weingarten, Bette Ziegler.

To the women in Dialogue, a support network that has shown enthusiastic encouragement and tender concern.

To people who provided some of the leads and other information: Dr. Robert Adamson (director, College at Sixty), Gertrude Asher, Susan Babbit Brenner, Gladys Dobelle, Chris Filner, Elinor Fine, Louise Fisher, Lillian Kutscher, Jed Levine, New York Gray Panthers, Annette and Samuel Rosenblum, Linda and Stuart Rosenblum, Norman Sachs, Florence Leighton-Seskin, Abraham Tuchman, Marsha Vogel (project director, Foster Grandparent Program), Don Wigal.

To an efficient, conscientious typist, Jean Levine.

To Ann Tanenbaum, associate publisher of Newsweek Books, and Herbert Gilbert, managing editor, for their faith in this project. Also, my appreciation goes to Mary Ann Joulwan, who designed the book. Special thanks are extended to Janet Finnie; she has a rare insight and is a dedicated and spirited editor.

For Annette Shapiro Rosenblum

Mother of my soul, friend of my spirit

FOREWORD

At the age of thirty-five, I worry about growing older. I'm concerned about my future. I wonder what my life will be like in thirty years or more. And I find that many women of my generation share these same concerns.

Looking for reassurance and hoping for inspiration, I set out on a personal journey to find older women who might serve as role models—women who could offer options for our later years.

I began to explore the world of older women by leading discussion groups in two retirement homes. Through articles in newspapers and magazines, I learned of many women over sixty-five. The membership rolls of organizations and professional associations also provided leads. Friends gave me additional suggestions, as did friends of friends. As the names of hundreds of women crossed my desk, I began to feel there would always be one more woman with an interesting story to tell.

I was looking for women who had not let their chronological age stop them from growing personally and professionally. I was looking for women with a variety of living arrangements and lifestyles. I was also looking for women of different ethnic and religious backgrounds.

Of the many women who came to my attention, I selected more than fifty to approach by letter or telephone or both. Of these, twenty-two provided the interviews in this book.

The length of each interview ranged from two hours to seven. It might be one session or spread out over five meetings. All sessions were tape-recorded. In addition, many of the women filled out extensive questionnaires.

In a typical interview, I might ask thirty of my original list of eighty-seven questions. Here are some of them:

What factors in your earlier life have been most helpful to you in your present life?

Describe an average day. How do you spend your time?

What are your chief interests, your chief pleasures?

What do you consider your greatest strength? Your greatest weakness?

Do you recall one moment when you began to feel old?

What are the benefits of growing older? What do you feel free to do now that you didn't do when you were younger?

What, to your mind, is the most depressing thing about growing older?

There's a stereotype of older people as sexless. How do you feel about that?

What have you done in your life that you would change?

What do you think of the women's movement?

If everything were possible, how would you like to spend the rest of your life?

Have you made plans for a funeral? What would you like to have said about you at your funeral?

What are your feelings toward euthanasia? Toward suicide?

Do you have any advice for people younger than yourself?

How can someone prepare for later years?

The women presented in this book do not know one another. Most do not view themselves as role models, but just as women of a certain age. As one woman puts it, "Just because I'm eighty, I'm not an old lady. I just do less."

All of them think it is necessary to develop hobbies and interests during a person's young and midlife years. And the women agree that the best way to "feel young" is to keep physically and mentally active. They recommend joining groups, organizations and clubs, creating wider circles of friends and "doing for others." Time and again these women affirm their roles in life as participants rather than observers. A sixty-nine-year-old woman says, "I see my life as a pilgrimage and a growth process." Another, aged eighty, adds, "I used to think you *look* for happiness. Now I've decided you make and create your own." And a seventy-year-old author, who entered high school in this country without knowing a word of English, echoes this theme: "I function with daily persistence."

The women who successfully juggled home and career feel, in retrospect, that being a full-time mother during a child's early years is of prime importance. There is a consensus that today's children lack old-fashioned values and morals, and are raised "permissively" and "without adequate parental guidance."

Although the women share similar views on most topics, they sharply disagree when it comes to the women's movement. One woman describes women's liberation as the "best thing to happen since the wheel," while another sees it as "exaggerated and terribly destructive to the family structure."

They scoff at the idea that sex is incompatible with old age, and desire what most of us want in relationships: affection, warmth and kindness. The majority of them would like to have men in their lives, but bemoan "the lack of opportunity" to meet eligible men.

Another common thread is fear of dependency. These women place a high value on self-reliance and dignity. They do not wish to live with their children, to be viewed as an unnecessary burden or an unwelcome intruder. They do not want to be "useless," to "turn into a vegetable," or have to count on someone else for "a glass of water."

As they take control of their later years, they also make plans to control their futures. Some of them have prepared instructions for burial or cremation; written or selected an epitaph; even made plans for a "party." And one woman has written her own obituary.

These women have survived periods of personal loss, emotional depression, physical infirmity, religious or sexual discrimination. Yet they have done more than survive. They have coped with their pain, worked through their problems and grown stronger as individuals. They demonstrate many different ways to grow old. And perhaps that's the reassurance and inspiration I was looking for.

Older women *can* give us guidelines for our own lives if we will only talk to them, listen to them and learn from them.

And my own future, as I now realize, can be as rich and varied as I choose to make it.

JANE SESKIN

Marguerita Rudolph

AUTHOR AND EDUCATOR

For most of her life, Marguerita Rudolph has taught in and directed preschool and day-care programs. She is the author of more than thirty books for and about children. The latest, *Should the Children Know? Encounters with Death in the Lives of Children,* was published in 1978. Reviewers praised it as a "conscientious, finely tuned reference" and as an "outstanding source of advice."

She is seventy, a small woman with brown eyes. She is five feet tall. When I ask what she would change about herself, she replies, "My height"—and then laughs.

When we meet she is wearing a turquoise blouse, Mexican skirt and sandals. Her jewelry is silver. She keeps her short hair gray. "The only thing I do is color my eyebrows," she says. "When I looked in the mirror and saw my eyebrows getting gray, I couldn't stand it. I think of my eyebrows as a frame for my face."

Marguerita has lived since 1949 in her two-story attached house in Fresh Meadows, Queens, New York. There's a small porch in the front, and a larger terrace in the back opens out into a communal park. A round table holds two pots overflowing with rocks, part of her collection from all over the world.

Her house is cozily cluttered. Books, magazines and file folders are stacked in piles on the floor, on end tables and on chairs. Her desk occupies a prominent place in the small living room. Behind her cushioned chair, wall shelves are crammed with books. There are Mexican prints on the wall, multicolored pillows on the couch. The room *feels* lived in.

We talk here. I sit on the couch, with Marguerita in a rocking chair across from me. Then we move to the eat-in kitchen for a lunch of cold borscht, homemade bread and cheese.

Marguerita speaks English with a slight accent. Her tone is animated, her face frequently breaking into a warm, infectious grin. She laughs easily.

As the afternoon draws to a close, we walk across the park to the bus stop, where I'll catch the express bus back to Manhattan. "Am I walking too fast?" she asks as I hurry to keep up.

We pass a large tree with an odd assortment of wooden boards fastened to one of the limbs. She shakes her head. "A few little boys from the neighborhood are trying to build a tree house. Tomorrow I'll have to give them the right equipment."

In my hand I hold the rock she has given me as a memento of our visit. It's a comfortable fit.

You know, I'm going on seventy-one. I think "going on" is a very nice term, suggesting a positive approach. You're *going on,* not standing still. I was born in Russia and started school there. But my parents, who were bystanders, were killed in the Revolution. So as a teen-ager I came with relatives to Kansas. But first we were stopped at Ellis Island for almost three weeks. Since I was not yet sixteen, all kinds of guarantees were required. It was like being in a jail; a matron would come around at five o'clock in the morning and knock on your brass bed to wake you up. I remember all the time we spent standing in lines.

When I was in college I wrote an essay about being detained—and I won a fifty-dollar gold piece!

In Kansas I went to high school without knowing a word of English. I learned because I *had* to. And when people ask, "How did you become a writer?" I tell them, "Out of ignorance of the English language." In English, I was a deaf-mute illiterate. Well, you can't tolerate such a situation. So with all your resources, and all the urgency to emerge from that condition, you *learn*.

I don't like doing things on a regular basis. Habits get boring.

I don't like to be in any kind of trouble, so I get out of it as quickly as I can. Maybe it was a blessing that I was unable to use Russian in Kansas. But the culture and language remained in my consciousness. Now I am grateful, for I am able to do literary translations and more. Just last year I took a group of writers to Russia.

I worked my way through high school. I lived in a little attic room in a professor's home, where I kept house. I used to sing Russian songs as I vacuumed. The lady of the house was so eager to Americanize me that she made me stop whenever she heard me.

Everyone was very helpful. I had wonderful teachers, and the students were excused from their English classes to work with me. I became so interested in the language that I wanted to do more than learn it: I wanted to *master* it. I was the only foreigner, so I was a curiosity. I don't remember any derision, just warmth and helpfulness.

College, where I went on scholarship, was a pleasant, almost flighty time. I had lots of friends, and I made good enough grades, B's. College was more a social experience than a deeply intellectual one. But through one course and one professor I became terribly interested in young children. This was to become the focus of my teaching and my writing.

I received a fellowship to the University of Minnesota, at the Child Welfare Institute. I received free tuition, and they gave me a stipend of three hundred dollars and I lived on that. I don't remember suffering from it.

But I didn't get my master's degree. I was instead involved with deciding which of two men I should marry. I really think that at the time I wasn't intellectually mature enough to take advantage of the courses.

The man I chose to marry was also a student. He was a pianist, a chess champion. He was interested in many things. We saved up money and we went back to Russia in 1931. I was interested in what they were doing in child development. As it turned out, I got pregnant there. We decided that we didn't want the child to be brought up in a foreign country.

We came back—and it was a terrible time in this country for unemployment. Perhaps my husband's illness was due to that culture shock. He had delusions, and he couldn't hold a job.

He's been hospitalized since 1936. He's gone through periods when he's been subjected to shock treatments, insulin therapy, all kinds of programs that have come along since the thirties. I visit him about once or twice a year. When I know I'm going, it's already on my mind for days. He recognizes me but he has no sense of relating to anything. We'll play a modest game of chess. We'll talk about unimportant things.

As soon as I get home, I write his sister a full account of the day. I have copies of all those letters so I'll remember what it was like for me (by implication), and what he's like—what an insane person who's been hospitalized for so long is like.

If I wanted to remarry, then I'd get a divorce. However, when I inquired about doing something final or formal, I learned it would be a court procedure. What would be the sense of making him appear in court? If it were important, I guess I'd go through with it.

So I raised my daughter alone. I had to work. When she was small she was in my nursery-school group. One day she said, "I don't want you to be a teacher anymore. Just be a mommy."

I answered her and also myself when I said, "I like being a teacher. But when I am home with you, I will be just a mommy." I believed that. I didn't feel I was depriving her—and I didn't feel I was having a terrible life.

In some cases, if a woman is so miserable at home that she runs away to a job, and forgets her responsibilities, then that could hurt the family structure. Some escape, though, is necessary for everybody. It all depends on the method—books, movies, drink.

I finally got my master's at Bank Street College. While I was there, I met the educator Lucy Sprague Mitchell. I looked up to her intellectual prowess, admired her professional educational accomplishments, her literary originality, her glamorous personality. I was certainly influenced by her reactions to my writing when she founded and led the Writers Laboratory at Bank Street. There were a group of us who began with her in 1939. My first children's book, a supplementary book used in grade schools, was very well received. It was my story of being brought up as a peasant in a Ukrainian village.

I also began to write a lot of magazine articles—fifteen dollars here, ten dollars there. It wasn't enough to live on, but the writing supplemented my teaching salary. I wrote at night, on weekends, during school holidays, and during the days I worked with and learned from children.

Everyone said to me, "You haven't changed at all." Perhaps they saw a presentation of my inner self which transcends the external physical changes—the wrinkles, the gray hair.

While I was writing one book, I substituted in nursery schools. A child said to me, "You're old. You're going to die." That was a statement of fact. It didn't really call for a reaction.

But I did answer him: "Yes, I am old. And I'm a grandmother." I think I said that to justify my age. But I didn't really have to say anything. Today there are many books that give children a positive image of old age. Children will learn to regard older people the way society regards them.

Unfortunately there isn't much contact between young children and old people unless it's artificially provided. Most grandmothers no longer live at home.

Should parents live with their grown children? It has to be a tradition; otherwise it's intolerable. If it's a tradition, you don't question: you do it and make the best of it.

I love living *near* my daughter, Alicia, and her family. My grandsons and I have a unique relationship. I'm fascinated by the two of them. They give me a sense of fulfillment and richness.

Alicia and I have similar interests; that's probably why we have such a good relationship. I've learned a lot from her. For instance, she knows what colors go together; sometimes she'll shop for me, buy clothes without my being there. She's also a marvelous cook. I'll come home, and she'll have left some wonderful casserole.

When you get older it's important to derive some pleasure from your family. If you have that, then you're free to reach out to the rest of the world.

From children I learned to be curious—to investigate my immediate environment, to learn what's underfoot. I collect rocks, piles and piles of them, from all over the world. A machine is a machine is a machine, but the rocks you pick up are all *different*. I pick up stones that fit in my hand, that feel good, that people give to me.

I write every morning, sometimes into the afternoon, but I'm no good in the evening. First I do a rough draft in longhand, then a rough typed draft when I revise. If I get stuck on a particular section, page or idea, I put it away while I work on something else.

I don't take regular vacations; if I go away I find that after two days I want to get back to work. For the winter term I go to Mexico, to the Instituto Allende. In exchange for a beautiful apartment right on the campus, I teach a class in creative writing and give a few lectures. I go from December through the middle of March. I do a lot of my writing there because I always seem to be meeting a deadline. There's a beautiful natural-spring pool where I swim every day.

As far as teachers go, most of them are pedestrian. Teaching young children demands not only serious effort but dedication. It exhausts you. You need a chance to share with adults. I think a good teacher constantly assesses her own efforts. Seeing her faults, she won't perpetuate them.

I think this applies to writing too. Sometimes I say to myself, "This is a terrible sentence." I'm so glad I see it so I can eradicate it. I think as you get older you don't become less critical. You become *more* critical as your judgment increases.

I've been lucky to have good health. Basically I don't think about it. I don't have colds because . . . maybe . . . I don't want them!

Last year I went into the hospital and got paid for it! It

was a hormonal study of women in later years. I was in for forty-eight hours. They took all kinds of tests. I was fascinated to learn some scientific facts along the way. They took my urine constantly; you can read it like a textbook. From the top of my skull they recorded my hormonal function as I slept, through the use of attached electrodes. The whole experiment was quite interesting, and I was paid seventy-five dollars.

I don't think of myself as an assertive person or a leader. I think I'm quite shy and quiet. I don't like organizing things or being pushy. I don't function with aggressiveness; I function with daily persistence.

I don't like habits—doing things on a regular basis. I call myself "unhabited." Habits get boring, and also I resent dependence on them. Some people must have a cup of coffee *every* morning before they get started. I like coffee, but if I don't have it, it doesn't bother me. Or I'll deliberately change my routine.

Last June I went to my fiftieth college reunion. It was a frivolous thing to do, but I was curious. There were a couple of hundred people there out of eight hundred in our class. I saw two of my beaus from 1929. They seemed to have held up pretty well. Yet I noticed the gait, the way some of the people walked, a little hunched over, a little bent. Their movement suggested advanced age.

Everyone said to me, "You haven't changed at all." Why, that's ridiculous! Of course I've changed. I wondered if they were just flattering me, or was their perception impaired? Perhaps they saw a presentation of my inner self which transcends the external physical changes—the wrinkles, the gray hair.

I prefer pleasure to pain. If you explore your advantages, you get much more out of life than if you dwell on the handicaps.

Now that you've asked, I will plan my own festive funeral with music, some original entertainment or performance, with a showing of slides of me in action and a recorded farewell.

When people grieve they really grieve for themselves. Their tears can't do the dead person any good because the body isn't suffering. Grieving is being sorry not for the person, but for yourself. You're saying, "I'm lonesome. I would be happier if you hadn't died. I'm crying for myself." Grief gradually leaves with time and with the demands of immediate concerns.

Euthanasia seems sensible in cases in which there is artificial prolongation of life, or useless and painful life with no prospect of recovery.

I'm optimistic. I used to feel apologetic about it, but I don't anymore. I feel I'm just as realistic in being optimistic as another person is in being pessimistic. And it's pleasanter. I prefer pleasure to pain. If you explore your advantages, you get much more out of life than if you dwell on the handicaps.

I love to bake. I find it's a very good complement to writing. The process of writing is cerebral, and the ideas you deal with are abstract. It is certainly sedentary. Any sensations or feelings are only evoked on the page. But baking has an active physical involvement, and it brings immediate results.

In writing you want to share with others. In baking one of the pleasures *is* in sharing—as in the phrase "breaking bread." It's a meaningful thing. If I haven't baked for a couple of weeks I miss it. When guests come I like to bake something special as a way of welcoming them to my house.

Since we're on the subject of food and this really is part of things physical, I prefer to eat the whole orange. Your hands are involved. It's a sensory experience. Drinking juice is just taking it down, from outside to inside. I hate even to throw away the peel. So I stick it in the coffee. It gives a nice flavor.

I used to do yoga with television at six-thirty in the morning. Then the show got canceled. But I found you can do the motions, bends and stretches as you move around the house. I purposely put my dishes on a high shelf so I'll have to stretch and reach for them. After you come out of the shower, when you dry yourself with a towel, there's an opportunity to use different movements. You make your own exercises, your own balance.

There was no specific incident when I first felt I was getting old—not graying hair, not cessation of menstruation, not appearance of belly bulge. . . . Well, perhaps, when I was in my sixties and heard an active, attractive male acquaintance *my own age* say derisively, "Can you imagine me going to bed with a *sixty-year-old* woman?"

I haven't yet suffered discrimination because of age— but I haven't been applying for a job. Editors have no such discrimination against authors. And I feel that my many friends, most of whom are younger, certainly don't slight me because of age. In fact some think my age is a plus!

If I were younger I'd learn Spanish with ease (instead of struggling). I would become a competent driver (instead of a scared nondriver). And I would *look* beautiful, with smooth skin, agile limbs, exuding freshness. However, when I *was* young, I wasn't happy with my appearance. And now that I am old, I cannot complain about looks— for I don't mind gray hair, and I am getting used to wrinkles.

Being an optimist I don't actually fear getting still older. I realize that it's inevitable, and that there will be lessened energies and change of pace, no doubt. I already walk slowly up subway steps. I wouldn't want to be as debilitated and helpless and semiabandoned as old people sometimes are. However, I don't think this will happen to me. The worst that could happen would be to become useless. That would be embarrassing!

Older people aren't sexless. Society's got the notion

*I don't care anymore what kind of
impression I'm making. It's good enough
to be. I don't have to appear any special
way.*

that youth has everything, that sex is youth, that sex is only
a particular biological function. With a person of the opposite sex you can have a relationship that transcends genital sex. There's a give-and-take, flirtation, affection. The
word "sex" is used so loosely. "Having sex," people say.
You don't *have* sex. That sounds so ugly. It repels me.

Older people may not want to speak out because they
don't want to make fools of themselves. I used to have terrible stage fright. I feel more confident because I don't
care anymore what kind of impression I'm making. It's
good enough to *be*. I don't have to *appear* any special way.

People don't have to be lonely. Look around for something important to do, something meaningful—for yourself or for others. You won't be lonesome if you're helping
someone. If you listen to somebody else's troubles, they
may make you realize you're better off.

I think people waste their time by *not* doing things. They
should *use* themselves. If they did, if everyone used all
their skills, we'd be way ahead.

I've been considering a new career: I think storytelling
would be a becoming occupation for an old lady. I've tak-
en some seminars, and I've already tried telling stories to
children in Central Park. I enjoyed it. You're facing an audience, and you're working up the effect. There's a kind of
directness. It's completely different from writing—another
form of communication.

When I'm seventy-five, I'm planning to have a big birthday party with lots of people. It will be outdoors, and everyone will bring food. It should be fun. It's something to
look forward to, yes?

Fanny Rosenau

VOLUNTEER COORDINATOR
REACH TO RECOVERY

The American Cancer Society has its own building on West 56th Street in Manhattan. Fanny Rosenau's office is on the third floor. She is in charge of the Reach to Recovery program for New York City women who have had mastectomies. Fifty-two hospitals in the metropolitan area use the services of Reach to Recovery; by the end of 1978 the program had cared for 2,290 patients.

Fanny Rosenau is eighty-two years old. Her office is different from most. In addition to framed prints on the walls and plants on the windowsill, there is a rack of bathing suits—"to show the women they can wear what they wore before"—and two upper-torso models wearing white cotton bras. "In this room," says Fanny, "I have a complete display of all the commercial breast pads on the market. We let the women know what's available. You know the saying: 'An educated consumer is the best customer.' "

The office also contains a chart showing how to examine your breasts, a shelf of books on the subject of cancer, many photographs of Fanny taken with celebrities

who support the American Cancer Society and two certificates of appreciation presented by the society's national board.

Fanny is tall, gray-haired, solidly built. She radiates
strength. In a simply tailored gray sheath dress,
adorned only by gold jewelry, she is a woman of stately
elegance.

She wears only one earring, the other removed as a
convenience for answering the constantly ringing telephone. While I am in her office, she answers incoming
inquiries about adjustment to a husband, to children;
about where to buy a bathing suit; about dealing with an
uncaring doctor. Her voice is alternately soothing,
forceful and commanding.

*B*eing the volunteer coordinator for the Reach to
Recovery program in the area has for me many
rewards. This is short-term rehabilitation for
women who've had mastectomies. I had a mastectomy thirty-three years ago, never have had a recurrence,
and was instrumental in starting this program before it
hooked up with the American Cancer Society. Mrs. Terese
Lasser and I worked it out together.

Terese became the national coordinator of the program,
and I'm in charge of New York City. It's a full-time job, believe me. Today we have eighty-seven volunteers in New
York City hospitals. My main interest is the woman in the
hospital. I want to extend my hand figuratively to a Mrs.
Smith who underwent surgery four days before and may
feel ready to shoot herself.

It's my job to arrange for volunteers to visit patients in
hospitals near their homes or jobs. The doctor must re-
quest the visit to the patient in the hospital. After Mrs.
Smith has recovered and the doctor says she's ready for a
permanent prosthesis, we hope she'll come in here to my
office.

I much prefer the hospital work to the office work. I took this job with the understanding that the hospital work would come first. I just feel much more effective there.

When there's a patient to visit in a hospital in my neighborhood, the secretary here calls me up with all the information: the name of the patient, and the hospital she's in. I have a supply of kits at home.

The hell with the label. Call me a dirty old lady if you want. It wouldn't bother me at all.

After I get to the hospital, I speak to the charge nurse: "I'm here to see Mary Smith. Is there anything you'd like to tell me about her?" And sometimes there is. For instance, Mary may have bursitis on her left side where her mastectomy was performed. Under no circumstances is she to do any exercises that day; so then I know that I'll only demonstrate them. Or Mary Smith's husband may be a son-of-a-gun. He hasn't been a bit nice, and she's crying all the time because her husband hasn't been attentive. I want to know the areas where I shouldn't say the wrong thing.

Then I go in to Mary Smith—with a smile. I try not to come on too strong because some people, fourth or fifth day post-op, can't take that. I tell Mary that her doctor suggested I see her; that I've had the same surgery she's had; and that I've brought her a present. "Here it is," I say. "And it doesn't cost you a cent."

I show her the kit, which contains a temporary breast pad, a brassiere for her to wear home, a book for her to read, a ball and a rope for exercise. I tell her I'll demonstrate the exercises and that I'll answer any questions she might have.

I usually stay about an hour. However, some women are not responsive. If that's the case, I get in and get out. I've been thrown out of hospital rooms by women who weren't ready to see anyone. But six to eight weeks later they'll come in here to apologize.

I have been horrified in the last year to see how many young women are having mastectomies in their late twenties and early thirties. In my opinion, the best thing friends and family can do is to act natural. The mastectomy patient is the same woman she was before. If it was her eye that was removed, God forbid, or a finger, they'd treat her as she'd been before. The importance of the breast has been exaggerated in our Western culture. It's chiefly there to nurse a baby!

If a woman wants to become a volunteer for Reach to Recovery, she must wait a year after her mastectomy. We get a group together, here in the office, and we train them all at once. The training involves the women in a number of role-playing situations.

After my mastectomy, I was scared to death. I was sure my husband was going to leave me for a blonde. I was sure I'd never live to raise my three children. I was sure I was going to die. Why wouldn't I be scared? I still get scared when I go to the doctor twice a year to examine my other breast; I don't get off the toilet all morning.

I was fortunate that my doctor was a personal friend. He took tender loving care of me—far better than if I were with a strange surgeon whom I didn't know and had questions about, and whom I couldn't talk to. I could ask my doctor anything. It made a big difference to me.

Friends were scared; they didn't know what to say. They didn't want to come around and see me. It was awful.

But my husband was superb. During the first month I wouldn't let him near me. I used to dress and undress in the bathroom. And I guess I was angry that he didn't say anything.

One evening I said to him, "What are you doing, laying a broad downtown?"

And he said to me, "It's your fault, honey. I've been afraid to come near you."
And that ended that.

The importance of the breast has been exaggerated in our Western culture. It's chiefly there to nurse a baby.

I have a feeling that nothing in the long run helps you but yourself. This is my real gut feeling. We can extend a hand to a woman over the first hurdle. But in the last analysis—and this is true not only of mastectomies but of anything—you've got to do it yourself. I've got guts. I had a supportive loving husband and three gorgeous children, and they were all there. I didn't have to worry about where the next penny was coming from. I had everything going for me. But I still could have been a basket case.

When I was very young, I read a book by Hugh Walpole, and there's one sentence I've never forgotten. I wrote it in my notebook in school, and when my first grandchild was born, I embroidered it on a sampler for her. He said: "It isn't life that matters, it's the courage you bring to it." You have to solve things yourself. You can go to psychiatrists; I'm sure they help. But in the end you determine your own fate.

Eight years after my mastectomy, I met Mrs. Lasser in a corsetiere's shop. She was in one booth and I was in another. The corsetiere knew of Terese's interest in helping other mastectomy patients. Terese explained her idea to me. I thought, "Well, sure, my other volunteer work is important. But who is better able to counsel a mastectomy patient than a woman who has already gone through it?"

Terese and I struggled terribly—because the doctors didn't want us. When we first started, we asked the American Cancer Society just for a room and a telephone. They said, "No." Rehabilitation in those days meant an artificial arm or a leg. It didn't mean any psychological or cosmetic help for a woman with a mastectomy. Who talked about *breasts* twenty years ago? That was taboo; so was cancer. We worked out of our homes until Mount Sinai Hospital gave us a start. Finally the Cancer Society came to *us*. We joined up with them in 1969.

The nurses we've come into contact with have been wonderful; I've lectured at a lot of nursing schools. But some doctors are still resistant to the program. I don't know why; for twenty-five years I've asked myself that question. I don't want to think that it's their ego. I don't want to think they don't trust volunteers. I just don't know.

I'm a volunteer. I've never been paid for any of the work I've done since I married. Not only do I run this program for nothing, but I give money to it, too.

I was brought up to do volunteer work. My family in Philadelphia were always interested in it, and fortunately I can afford to do it. I've done it part-time all my life, so it was natural that when my children grew up I'd do it full-time.

I grew up in a loving home with devoted parents. I married the man my mother didn't want me to; that was my rebellion. And the only reason she didn't want me to was that he didn't have enough money and he was two years younger than I was. After we got married, as soon as he became successful and made money, my mother thought he was marvelous.

I've had a happy life, so why shouldn't I do something for other people? All my life I saw people giving. My mother was a darling woman, social and not very bright, but loving, and she gave what she could. My only sister, who lives in Chicago, started a branch of the American Diabetes Association some years ago, and is still with them.

My mother's best friend, Cora Arnold, ran a girl's camp.

Cora influenced me very much because she treated me as a growing human being and *not* as a little girl. She was never married, a real career woman; there were not many in those days. She inspired me to *do* things! My loving mother only wanted me to get married to a man of *her* choice. Cora encouraged me to *do*—to go to college and to work afterwards.

I think the women's movement has gone overboard in some areas. What worries me most in my own field is the feeling that unconsciously the women's movement has made women antagonistic to their surgeons.

A woman no longer trusts the man who's operating on her. After a biopsy, she wants time to decide whether to have a mastectomy. What she doesn't realize is that it's not good to go under an anesthetic twice. If she would only put herself in the hands of a good doctor and have confidence in him and his ability! But these younger women won't do it, and that worries me very, very much. Accidents *do* happen under anesthesia.

Second opinions, of course, I can understand.

You have to solve things yourself. You can go to psychiatrists; I'm sure they help. But in the end you determine your own fate.

The women's movement certainly has done good; I don't dispute that. But I think it's been harmful to the family. Every woman now feels she must have a career. Yet I believe there's nothing more beautiful than having children, raising them, loving them and watching them grow.

That's my own opinion, for what it's worth. But this is all individual. You bring to every situation everything that's happened to you in your life. I was brought up in a gorgeous family, and I wanted the same for myself. I managed to do volunteer work on the side, but my family came first.

I guess the most important moment in my life was when I saw my first child. He didn't breathe. They had to put something up his nose or down his throat. Then he breathed and he yelled—and I never will forget it! And that was fifty-four years ago. Now he's a professor of political science, and I'm very proud of him.

I've had tragedies in my life. Besides losing my husband, I lost my only beautiful daughter at the age of forty-five. And a beautiful daughter-in-law was killed in an automobile accident. Both incidents were very traumatic. But I always went right back to work because you've got to live for the living, don't you? You can't allow yourself to dwell on past sorrows.

My daughter was ill with a kidney disease for a long time. After one kidney atrophied, it was removed. The doctors told her not to have children. After three years she said, "The hell with it. I want a baby." She had three babies in all. One day she was packing her own daughter's suitcase for college. She was sitting in a chair and just keeled over dead.

The *quality* of her life was beautiful, and that's really what was important, not the length of her life.

When my daughter died, I didn't shed a tear. You have to have broad shoulders. I've cried since—oh, a number of times—but not at that moment. I think I've had a happy life. That brings strength, don't you think?

My greatest pleasures are my eight grandchildren and my work. I see the kids in New York frequently, at least once a week. I feel grandparents shouldn't criticize, shouldn't tell the kids what to do. Grandparents should mind their own damn business.

When I visit *one* of the kids, I could almost die when I step into her apartment. It looks so messy that I can't even find a place to sit down. But I wouldn't say a word to her about it. I don't care what it looks like; I came to see her, not the state of her apartment. I enjoy being with her. She loves me; I love her. We talk a lot; we laugh a lot.

I have women friends whom I do things with: go to the theater or to the opera. But I miss a man very much. I guess I don't look for men. I don't seek them out. If I went out with a man, it would have to be someone with whom I could communicate on my level. And I wouldn't pay for his theater ticket either! The older women who've found men have gone after them with a vengeance. I don't like that sort of thing.

I'm up every morning at seven. I have a marvelous housekeeper, who's been with me for eighteen years. When I come home in the afternoon, I'm tired. I usually take a nap, read the paper, do the crossword puzzle, go out to dinner and play bridge, go to a concert, theater, whatever. I don't look at television except for the news.

You have to do what makes *you* happy. But I believe it's what's inside that counts. I have a friend who's had her face lifted three times. You have to do it again every few years because it starts to sag again. There's a smile on her face that she can't erase; she's absolutely wooden. Me, I like a little make-up.

I love beautiful clothes. When I went to the theater the other day, some of the young people in that audience looked disgusting. Their clothes weren't becoming. Women don't look attractive like women anymore, and men are beginning to look like women. I'm just old-fashioned, I guess.

I'd like to be thin, but I guess I'm not going to bother about that now. I wish the dressmakers and couturiers would make sizes eighteen and twenty instead of concentrating on sizes ten and twelve and six and eight. Let the old ladies who have to wear an eighteen be proud of it, and not squeeze themselves into a sixteen. Let a lady with a big behind wear something that suits her, and not a tight pair of shorts with her buttocks sticking out. That's just awful!

I haven't been discriminated against because of age—but because I was Jewish. This was when I was much younger. After graduating as a bacteriologist from the University of Pennsylvania, I went to get a job. The doctor I went to see, a Quaker, called up the University Hospital in Philadelphia. In those days the hospital was extremely anti-Semitic, but I didn't realize it.

The Quaker doctor said that he had someone qualified, and he mentioned my name.

The hospital doctor on the other end of the phone asked, "Is she Jewish?"

My Quaker friend replied, "Yes, she is."

The hospital doctor said, "We don't employ Jews in this laboratory."

I heard that on the telephone. It upset me no end, and it took a long time to get over it.

That was in 1920; Philadelphia was a very snooty place then. Now the University of Pennsylvania has a Jewish president, so times have changed.

I don't care what they call me—senior citizen, whatever. Labels don't mean anything to me. You're what you are—the hell with the label! Call me a dirty old lady if you want; it wouldn't bother me at all. I'm too secure. My years of experience in living a *full* life have given me, I feel, the privilege of saying what I think.

I feel grandparents shouldn't criticize, shouldn't tell the kids what to do. Grandparents should mind their own damn business.

What I fear most about growing older is being a burden to people because of the degenerative process of aging. I just pray that death comes quickly. I've told my children I don't want to be buried. I know where I'm going to be; my husband is up in a little box, cremated, and I'm going to be right next to him.

Oh, pooh! People shouldn't have to come to a funeral; people should have fun. I'll tell you, I'm for those who are left, not for those who are gone. I've had a beautiful life. When it's over, it's over, and I want my kids to go on. If people say something about me, "There goes a good gal" would be as good as anything.

I'm not a synagogue-going gal, but I do believe in a higher spirit than man. I've been well, and the only prayer I ever have is to give me courage. When my time comes, I hope I can face it with courage. Big talk!

Sure, age has its limitations. I'm not the woman I was twenty-five years ago—no question about that. I used to love to swim but now I have pains in my shoulders. I don't walk as much as I did because my legs aren't as good as they were.

That's about all, really. I still drive a car, and I travel. I took two of the grandchildren to Europe two years ago. We spent a week in Paris and a week in London. I was exhausted, and my feet hurt like hell—but we had a ball!

I'd want to give advice to the younger people, not to the old. Find a hobby, something you can really become involved in. Then, when you are older, you'll have a focus to your life. You won't just sit home and feel your arteries harden.

It's frightening to me that at this time, in this world, everyone is so self-centered. You've got to look outside yourself. I've had a saying in my notebook for years, a quotation from Emily Dickinson:

If I can stop one heart from breaking,
I shall not live in vain.
If I can ease one life the aching
Or cool one pain,
I shall not live in vain.

I work either here or in the hospital practically every day. If I've helped somebody over this hurdle of a mastectomy, then my day is made. I like to feel needed. This is really what I live for.

Four months later I call Fanny at her office. "It's good you called now, Jane, dear," says Fanny, "because I've just come back to work. I was in the hospital for four weeks. I had a slight heart attack, nothing to worry about. They tried to take away some of my piss and vinegar—but they couldn't!"

We talk about my recently published book, *Older Women/Younger Men*. Fanny says she would like "a man about fifty-two, handsome and rich." I tell her I'll put in the order.

Maxine Sullivan

Jazz Singer

Maxine Sullivan has enjoyed a long and notable singing career, with appearances at supper clubs, on the stage and on radio. A *New York Times* critic recently praised her "singing style that is both swinging and reserved. Although she maintains a cool, almost impassive presence, she sings with a light, lifting lilt that gives her work the rhythmic impetus that has been her hallmark."

To raise her children she took a ten-year self-imposed retirement from show business. She made a new name for herself as a community leader and organizer before returning to the night-club circuit as a singer. Last year at the age of sixty-eight she made another career switch, resulting in a nomination for the Broadway Tony award for "outstanding performance by a featured actress" in the musical *My Old Friends.*

Maxine and I meet in the communal dressing room she shares at the 22 Steps Theater on West 48th Street. I sit at her dressing table, which is crammed with cosmetics, mouthwash, fan letters, paper coffee cups and soda cans. I watch the black woman with the gray Afro, four

feet, eleven inches, ninety pounds, patiently taping and retaping a radio commercial promoting the show.

My Old Friends **is a charming, touching musical that portrays life in the Golden Days Retirement Hotel. The opening song, performed by the hotel's eight residents, includes these words: "Old is twenty years older than I am today."**

After the Wednesday matinee, Maxine and I share a long lunch. We walk around the theater district on a beautiful spring day. And we talk.

lthough I never considered myself an actress, it's sort of a crazy feeling to wind up getting a Tony nomination for "outstanding performance as an actress" when I'm basically a singer. I must say I'm getting quite a bang out of my work.

Back in Homestead, Pennsylvania, where I was born, I always sang. It was part of everyday growing up. We had a phonograph (in those days it was a Victrola) and a lot of records and a player piano. My father was one of ten children who all played some kind of instrument—the back-porch variety. My father, who was a barber, played the mandolin.

In 1925 I won a Charleston contest, and the prize was an appearance at a local movie house. About four times a day, in the twenty minutes between showings of the movie, I'd go out there and do my dance.

When I got older I sang at a lot of local places. Then, when I decided to take singing seriously, I had a difficult time getting a job because my voice was so soft; this was way back before microphones. In the clubs you needed a big voice, and I just wasn't making it.

In 1936 I was singing with my uncle's band, the Red Hot Peppers. He had a friend who worked in Pittsburgh at the Benjamin Harrison Literary Club. It was a private club with about eight tables. The night before I was to audition there, there was a serious flood that went up to the second floor. The audition had to be postponed for months.

I finally got the job. I was twenty-six. The idea was to sing at the tables and bring back tips. I was bringing back small change—you know, the rattling kind. So I was a little worried because the salary was fourteen dollars a week plus tips, and you split the tips with the piano player, and I got the notion that she wasn't too happy.

That was really my first professional job. The hours were from eleven till unconscious. It was a good start for my career because it was an after-hours club. The legal time for closing was two o'clock, and most of the musicians in Pittsburgh showed up to eat and to drink and to have some fun. Because I happened to be there, I got a lot of encouragement from them.

Gladys Mosher, the piano player with Ina Ray Hutton's All-Girl Band, dropped in one night. She told me, if I ever came to New York, to look her up. So I started saving my money, and a year later I tried to find Gladys Mosher. I was lucky that she was even in New York at that time; I found her playing at the Paramount Theatre.

I said, "Hi, this is Maxine Williams." That's who I was at the time.

She said, "Maxine who?" But then she remembered who I was, and said she'd see what she could do. She contacted Claude Thornhill, who at the time was an arranger for André Kostelanetz. Later Claude formed his own band.

I was staying in Harlem then, and I must have auditioned in every club from 155th Street down to 52nd Street. Finally I got a job at the Onyx Club, which in those days was known as "the cradle of swing."

Claude decided on my name change: I became Maxine Sullivan. He was also responsible for the arrangement of "Loch Lomond" which made me famous. He did the recording, too. Our "Loch Lomond" became a hit, an international sensation. It was new—the idea of swinging a traditional song.

And what really capped it was a program on CBS radio called "The Saturday Night Swing Club." I sang our version of "Loch Lomond." The network station manager in Detroit cut it off the air because, he said, it was sacrilegious to swing a traditional folk song! I'm not kidding! This was in 1937.

So the next week they arranged to have a so-called "showdown." In Detroit they had Ray Heatherton, Rïse Stevens, a large choir and a large orchestra. In New York, I sang two songs, "A Brown Bird Singing" and "Loch Lomond," with a six-piece combination in a small studio. The others did the arrangements as they thought they should be done. The network switched to New York to do my version, and then they switched to Detroit to do theirs. Lots of people argued about the two versions. The controversy seemed to run forever.

By thirty-five I think you should be on some kind of track. You ought to know where you're going by that time. If you don't, then you've got to take what comes.

Loch Lomond is a lake in Scotland, twenty-four miles long. I went there on a tour about 1948. There was a tremendous amount of press coverage because our version was still an oddity. I've gotten a lot of mileage out of "Loch Lomond." When I went to Hollywood, I sang it in the movie *St. Louis Blues*. Oh, boy, I sang "Loch Lomond" so much it was coming out my ears!

I made another picture, *Going Places*, with Louis Armstrong. And then I toured clubs; I did vaudeville; I did a lot of concerts.

In 1957 I retired from professional singing after twenty years. My daughter was coming out of elementary school, going into junior high school, and I decided I wanted to stay home. So I became involved in the community. I joined the Parents Association and became its president. Everyone knew me as Mrs. Williams; I don't think anyone there had ever heard of Maxine Sullivan. I sang only once a year: at the Parents Association meeting, I'd get up on a chair and sing "The Star-Spangled Banner."

Then I became chairman of the local school board in my district. I didn't sing at all. I didn't think that I could do both. I was just as interested and sincere about working in the school system as I had been about my singing career. As for the singing—well, I could always sing around the house. I was retired for ten years without making any personal appearances. Meanwhile my husband Cliff, a piano player, was right downtown where the action was.

Then in 1967 a club opened in Washington called Blues Alley. I got a call asking me to sing there.

I said I couldn't appear; I wouldn't be available until school closed in June.

Later I got another call saying, "You open July the twelfth."

So I said, "Okay, why not?"

I did go down to Washington and I did open. It was a nice little club. I saw a lot of people I'd seen through the years, and it made me feel good.

In 1969 I still wasn't sure whether I should go back to my career or not. You know: "Maybe it's later than I think to be getting back into show business." So I was a little scared. But I joined the World's Greatest Jazz Band. We toured London, Germany, Denmark, Holland and Sweden on extended engagements. We've been going back to the Atlantic Club in Stockholm for the last three years.

When I decided to go back, Paula, my daughter, was getting ready to graduate—and I wasn't going to be found sitting around in a rocking chair. Cliff being a musician, he understood. They were probably wondering when I was going to get back in anyway.

I feel very good about singing to a live audience because I can sense the reaction. My repertoire consists mainly of standards, songs that everybody knows, and I really get quite a kick seeing how the audience reacts to the songs. Sometimes they even hum along. I usually do a first chorus straight, the way it was written, and then improvise on the second chorus by singing around the melody.

I get to the theater a half-hour before curtain. But in a club I try to get there at least an hour or so before—just because I like to be on a job early. I usually have to give my music out to the musicians, or I may have to explain a few things. I might have a vodka-and-tonic before I go on, but that isn't a requirement. I think all performers are nervous before they go on, standing in the wings, you know, waiting to be announced. But once you get out there, you lose your nervousness.

I'm not as cool as I look. I don't perspire, and I don't sing with much outward effort, but I'm working hard. Some people, when they work, put everything out. When I work, people say I'm so cool, so relaxed. Well, I'm bleeding internally; I'm suffering inside.

When I went into *My Old Friends,* I guess it was to add another dimension to my career, to get the experience, to learn a little bit. Working with a director like Phil Rose, you have a lot of opportunity to do things on your own. He's not the kind of director who has everything all mapped out for you, like "Walk over there." You do what comes naturally. If it looks good, that's it. This gives the performer an opportunity to exercise some creative ability instead of just being a robot walking across the stage.

Someone interviewed me for a book about 52nd Street, *The Street That Never Slept.* I told him, "See, there's still a little starch left in the old girl yet." And that's where the songwriters for *My Old Friends* got the idea for one song in this show—just from that one line.

This part of Mrs. Cooper in *My Old Friends* required me to do the mambo, and I said I couldn't do that. But I did!

It was just going to be twelve performances Off Off Broadway. I thought it would be an experience—you know, something of a lark. But I didn't realize you had to be available to rehearse! I was still doing some jazz concerts. I was also organizing a benefit for a jazz center I founded, the House That Jazz Built. So I was plenty busy. Then *My Old Friends* moved to the Orpheum Theater downtown, and now we're on Broadway.

I doubt I'll get married again. I like my independence. I don't think it would be very easy for anybody to get along with me these days because I'm not willing to make any sacrifices.

The House That Jazz Built has been in operation since 1974, in the South Bronx. I'm the founder and director. The purpose of the center is to promote jazz in the community. We have a summer program for kids, who come for lunch and listen to traditional jazz records. We try to teach them that what they're listening to is not new—that jazz has roots and a heritage. We also take the kids on trips to see actual jazz sessions in progress.

The fact that I'm tied up with the show allows me to delegate responsibility to the board members of the House That Jazz Built. In between shows, I do mailings and plan programs—a lot of paperwork.

In the backyard of the house, the seniors in the neighborhood planted a garden. People in the South Bronx seemed despondent, powerless. This gave them something to do. Politicians come and go, but these people live there. Of course, I live there too, in the South Bronx, a block away from the House That Jazz Built.

I've been married three times. I was married to a band leader when I first moved to New York. We were apart so much of the time that we just went different ways. My second husband was a doctor. I stayed home for a while and tried to be a housewife, but that didn't work out. So I went back to work. I guess my environment and his environment just didn't go together.

My last marriage was to Cliff Jackson, the piano player, and we were together for twenty years. So that one worked. He died in May of 1970.

I doubt I'll get married again; I'd be afraid to be tied down. I'm doing all right, and I like my independence. I don't think it would be very easy for anybody to get along with me these days because I'm not willing to make any sacrifices.

I've had some very close friends, but in the last years I've lost quite a few of them. I live pretty much alone, and I don't socialize too much. When I'm not working, I spend most of my time at home trying to get things done. I crochet, knit, make some of my own clothes. Since I'm so small I have trouble getting clothes to fit me. In size threes and size fives, the styles are too young for me. I like something that's simple and comfortable to sing in. So I end up with jump suits and slacks and tops.

My daughter, who is thirty-four, is a nurse. She's pretty busy and very dedicated. I ask her a lot of things about my health, but all she says is, "Go to a doctor." She's a lovely girl, married, a good housekeeper and a good cook. There are times when we see each other quite frequently, about once a week, and then sometimes I don't see her for months. But I talk to her all the time on the phone.

My son is fifty-one. He's a musician, a piano player. He's a bachelor, and he lives with me. He's somewhat of a pain in the neck—but not really. It's good to have him around. The house is comparatively big; I've lived there thirty-three years, and now there are just the two of us.

Advice? You've just got to hang in there. What the heck,

what looks bad today is not going to look bad tomorrow. Try to work it out. But you can only do one thing at a time; some people are in too much of a hurry. I say to myself, "Okay, okay, hold it. Tomorrow's another day."

I'm no sage, but by thirty-five I think you should be on some kind of track. If you don't know where you're going by that time, you've got to take what comes. Of course you can learn more along the way. But don't say, "Well, I *should* have this or I *should* have that." You have to work at what you think is important and then try to get it. I'm a long-range planner. I pick out a goal—and then I know there are some things that I have to do to get there.

I've found out, if there's something I can't do anything about, why fret myself about it? After you've got to a certain age and you've seen quite a few things, you just don't get upset so easily about something that doesn't concern you. If I see something disturbing in the paper, I just turn the page.

I think the mandatory retirement age is ridiculous, especially because people are living longer. I can remember when forty-five was supposed to be old; when I first started singing I was looking forward to my own retirement at forty-five! There are a lot of older people who are quite active and doing different interesting things. If people get involved in other things, their problems diminish. I don't know whether this is an escape or what—but, if it is, it works for me.

I might one day, in the not-too-distant future, decide to go into one of those resident homes. I'm worried that it might be too regimented with all those programs, hour by hour. On the other hand, I don't suppose you have to participate in everything. You're not in jail.

The only time I think about dying is when I have a sharp pain in my stomach. I don't believe you're going to die and then come back; I believe that you're never gone and you're always here. If people want to have a ball at my funeral, that's okay with me. In fact, I think it would be great if it was a happy occasion, no tears. I don't know what I'd like people to say about me. If I went now I'd be going out in a blaze of glory; let's keep it that way.

If I had a terminal illness I think I'd go on being active until I dropped. If I found out I had cancer I definitely wouldn't do anything about it. If I suffered a lot I'd want drugs to relieve the pain, but I wouldn't want to be cut, and I wouldn't want to undergo all kinds of treatments. I'm going to go anyhow, sooner or later. I wouldn't be afraid.

I believe in challenges. When there's nothing to challenge you, then I believe life stops.

I can't conceive of parents living with their married children. The difference in the younger people's lifestyle and the older people's lifestyle has grown considerably. Sometimes it appears that everybody's getting along okay, but underneath a lot of things might be boiling.

Older people can give nothing to the younger generation if the younger generation doesn't want it. On the other hand, if older people don't warrant respect, then they shouldn't demand it. I think that there's too much stereotyping of both age groups; the older people think the younger people stink and vice versa. If they got together more often they'd find they had a lot in common. Whatever the problems are, they could work them out together.

Younger people are trying to do in a week what takes years. Older people have already had all the problems. How they've faced them or coped with them—that's a part of the sharing they can give to younger people. They could say, "Well, look, you'll get over this. Take your time. Things do change. This is the way I overcame my problem. Try it." Older people are everywhere; all the younger people have to do is reach out.

Happiness is being able to do most of the things you want—and, when you run into a snag, being able to get out of it.

I believe in challenges. When there's nothing to challenge you, then I believe life stops.

Angelina Boccaccio

Foster Grandparent

The Foster Grandparent program is fifteen years old. It is the first federally approved program to offer "a retirement *to* instead of a retirement *from*." Foster Grandparents are parent substitutes for children who lack normal relationships with parents or grandparents. The program helps children in pediatric wards of hospitals; in homes for the dependent and neglected; in institutions for the mentally retarded, emotionally disturbed or physically handicapped.

There are approximately ten thousand Foster Grandparents working in the program in the fifty states, Puerto Rico and the Virgin Islands. They must be at least sixty years old and in good health. They receive forty hours of orientation and training. Each receives an annual stipend of $1,670, carfare allowance, a daily hot lunch, a free annual physical examination, complete accident-insurance coverage, as well as paid vacation, holidays and sick days. In New York, the program has been sponsored since 1973 by the Department for the Aging.

Angelina Boccaccio, seventy-eight, has been a Foster Grandparent for five years. She works at the Manhattan Developmental Center in Greenwich Village, a fifty-minute commute ("if the trains are running on time") from her home in Brooklyn. The center is operated by New York State for developmentally disabled children and adults. It is located near the docks of the Hudson River in an area known for warehouses and packaging plants.

The center's reception area is staffed by two uniformed security women. After signing in, I meet Judy Trent, the director of volunteer services. To bring the elevator down to the main floor, she inserts her key in a switch. This security measure is a holdover from a time when the center housed drug addicts. Now it discourages the residents from wandering away. The building houses 130 people from eleven to sixty years old. Miss Trent's office, a small room with cinder-block walls, holds a desk, gray file cabinets and two armchairs.

Angelina, who is waiting for me, wears a red housedress and white nurse's shoes. Her wavy gray hair is pulled away from her face by a black headband. Her brown eyes are friendly and alert behind her glasses. She often smooths her dress, her eyes darting to the floor before answering my questions. There is no hesitation as she speaks, although she frequently states, "This is only my opinion. You can't judge others by me. Maybe I shouldn't say this."

*M*y mother was American, born in 1881. I'm the oldest of ten brothers and sisters. She was raised and educated in New York City. You couldn't say anything bad about the city.
I lived on a farm for ten years until my mother got restless. I can remember hearing her tell my father, "These girls have got to get off this farm. They've got to go to

work." That's all we heard at home: work, work, work. And one day, soon after that, she packed us up and we moved to the city.

When I met my husband I was working as a decorator in a lampshade company. He had a fruit store nearby. Because I love my fruit, I went in there every day. I knew him a year and a half before we went out on a date. But, boy, did we have some good conversations!

Then I resigned from my job. When I went back for my pay, I went into his store.

He said, "I've missed you. Have you been ill?"

When I told him I had resigned, that he wasn't going to see me again, he took my phone number. The rest you might call history.

You think you know life, but when they put a baby in your arms everything changes. The world looked entirely different to me. I can still see my husband's face when he came in to see me: it was beautiful. I didn't want to work; I felt, to raise a child right, you had to be home. You had to stay on top of things.

I don't understand what women want today. I think the man is the backbone of the country and of the home. That's the way I was brought up. I wouldn't put the apron on a man because that would make him putty.

My husband's business failed during the Depression. By that time I had gone back to work. He used to get up at four in the morning to look for a job; he felt very bad that I was working and making nice money and he wasn't. Finally he started his own company. We used my salary to help pay his workers. When the boys were growing up, I kept all his books until he could afford to hire an accountant. No one had to force me because I *wanted* to help him.

We were married for fifteen years. He passed away a week after our anniversary. I never remarried. It didn't appeal to me; I guess it didn't dawn on me to even try. I was too preoccupied raising my two sons. I had too much to do.

I don't know what women want. I think the man is the backbone of the country and the home.

Sex didn't enter my mind. Maybe that goes back to my mother, who said, "If you keep yourself real busy, then you're so damn tired that it isn't going to bother you." My mother didn't believe in idleness.

I think the children of today are being raised too permissively. I blame the mothers. If they're bored and frustrated, they go to bingo or they play cards. But children need guidance, a firm hand.

I couldn't live with my married children because we're different in our ways. I have one daughter-in-law who's terrific but can't work with the clock. Now, me, I'm punctual to a fault. If I want her for dinner at three o'clock, I have to say two. Then she'll be there at three. I couldn't live like that! I need a routine; I need a schedule; I need to work.

I was fifty-four when I went to work at the Chase Manhattan Bank, running an IBM machine. I did that while my son was going to night school. Chase was having trouble getting women for the night shift, from five-thirty to twelve-thirty. Well, that was perfect for me. I worked there ten years. In all that time I only missed twelve days.

I wasn't afraid going home so late—except once. It was about one in the morning. I always walked near the curb because it's safer that way. I was heading toward the subway train, minding my own business. A man started following me; I could hear him crunch in the snow. Then he was walking right next to me. He said, "My, you have such beautiful legs." Well, I ran back like a demon was chasing me! It was a half-block to the subway, but two blocks to the bank. I was so crazy that I ran back to the bank!

My mother, when she was ninety-one, would scold me if I had nothing to do with my time. This was in September 1974, right before she died. She'd say, "You're wandering around like a chicken whose head's been cut off its neck. Don't you have a piece of material to work on? Sew something. Make an apron. Don't tell me you have nothing to occupy you."

And, you know, she was right. I have a garden, front and back, and I have eight rooms. Yet I had nothing to do, and I felt something was missing. My daughter-in-law told me about the Foster Grandparent program.

One morning I woke up and said to myself, "What the hell am I doing here?" So I decided to talk to the director, Mrs. Vogel. I should have called to make an appointment, but I got right on a train and went to her office. I decided I'd just stay there till someone talked to me. I said, "I want a job." I was lucky that Mrs. Vogel wasn't too busy to see me. I really believe there was an inner force at work.

We had a good orientation program. It included ways to take care of and teach the developmentally disabled child. For instance, we learned the best way to teach the child to feed himself. We learned how to teach sounds and words by imitation and by demonstration. And we learned how to help these children with their special problems.

I make them talk, and I make them walk. I teach them how to wash their faces. I take them to the toilet. I teach them how to clean themselves. If they have bad habits, like picking their nose, I try to break them of that.

According to the rules, you're just supposed to stick with one child. But, if I see that someone needs help with another child, I pop right in. You can't go by the rules all the time.

I get here at ten in the morning and leave around three. I go into the classroom and sit with the child. I do whatever the teacher wants. If the child already knows what's being covered, I can go on with something else.

After a while you understand your child. You know if he's not well from the expression on his face, the look of his eyes. You can tell all that if you pay attention. If he can't talk, you get to *know* when he wants a drink, so you take him to the fountain. Or you *know* when he needs to move his bowels. You also have to *know* when the child has had enough. A normal child can sit for a period of time, but ours begin to act up. When that happens, you just take him out of the situation and go for a walk.

I need a routine. I need a schedule. I need to work.

For a long time I had Tommy M., who was hyperactive. He had such mysterious eyes! We had a routine. He'd go to the bathroom; then we'd go out for a walk; then I'd give him an apple. He was a good boy and we made quite a lot of progress. I felt badly when he moved.

I had Paulette for four years. She was autistic. When she was three, she was placed in a home for the mentally retarded, so she *became* retarded as a result.

Paulette was able to talk when she was in the mood. I taught her how to eat with a knife and a fork. If she walked funny, I stopped her; I didn't want her to mimic other children. And, when we went outside, she never ran away from me. That had been a big problem with her, yet she clung to me like glue. She even learned to play the piano.

She understood firmness. I used to think that whoever heard me must think I'm some meanie! But I'm not. Paulette would come back to me, laugh and put her arms around me. I knew she understood what I'd said.

She was transferred to a foster home, and I hear she's doing beautifully. This month, she's going to be eighteen.

A good Foster Grandparent has to both like and love

the child. She's got to have a lot of patience, and she can't be easily ruffled. She mustn't let her emotions get out of hand so that she'd hit the child in anger.

The children love us. By and large they don't have families. We treat them as if they were our own—and they respond.

I've learned a lot here. If you have any kind of feelings at all, it makes you a better person. You realize how lucky you are. If I get depressed in the morning, I say, "Get up and go. The kids need you."

I have my day down to a routine. I'm up at six. I drink my coffee and get my bag ready for work. I take out my carfare, pass and keys; then I put my cereal on the stove. I go upstairs, make my bed, take my shower and get dressed. When I get back downstairs, I eat and then practice the piano for thirty minutes. I shut off my oil burner because you're supposed to save oil now. Then I grab my things and beat it.

I eat dinner between four-thirty and five because I'm better off not going to bed on a full stomach. I listen to the ten o'clock news, wash up and go to bed. I don't really like much TV. I watch musicals, and I love Lawrence Welk. And I love anything with Bette Davis.

I like current events because I like to know what's going on. If someone brings up a subject, I want to know I can talk about it. If I don't use my brain, I feel sick. But I don't want to read about murders. If I can't read something that's going to enlighten me, then I don't read it.

I took piano lessons as a girl. I wasn't allowed out on the street—the "mud gutter," we called it. My mother couldn't stand it if we fooled around; she wanted us to be inside, studying or practicing. I never wanted to play the piano professionally; I wanted the piano for *me*.

The piano stood unplayed for thirty-five years. It cost me two hundred dollars to get it back in shape. I went back to it because my fingers were stiff and I thought it would be good exercise.

I've learned a lot here. You realize how lucky you are. If I get depressed in the morning, I say, "Get up and go. The kids need you."

I'm a little bit of a loner. There's a Golden Age Club near my home where people go every Thursday from one to four. They pay a quarter for coffee and a piece of cake. I've got to pay to eat *their* cake? I can make my own!

But what's worse is when they play some kind of game. They play for a penny. You should hear them yell and scream and fight! I think these older people are selfish. They want to go and have the fun, but they all want to win all the time. And that's not possible.

If I go out and have to worry about the dollar, then I don't go. My husband taught me that. He said, "Never go out if you can't put your hand in your pocket. That's one of the worst things. But don't let anyone make a sucker out of you."

When I die, I'd like to go fast. The others, the ones you care about, are going to be suffering more.

My mother lost her sight after her menopause, so the radio became her world. But she was still very progressive, an intelligent woman. My mistake was believing she would get better. When she began to slip I held on too hard; I couldn't believe she would die. My brother admonished me when he came to visit. He said he thought I had better sense.

When I die I'd like to go fast. The others, the ones you care about, are going to be suffering more. I believe in God. I've never lost that faith. I think if you study the Bible you have a religion; you don't have to go to church to practice.

I'm going to be buried near my husband. I've discussed the plans with my son. He said, "Mama, I'm not going to have you three days in the funeral parlor. I'm going to have a memorial mass at the grave." After I'm dead, why should my sons have to pay those fees to the undertakers?

I think my family will miss me, especially my sisters. We're very close.

I don't know whether capital punishment is a cure. It's too easy to make mistakes. Once that life is gone, there's no way you're going to bring it back. Yet I remember my husband say, "If a tree doesn't bear fruit, you chop it down." So perhaps that's a moral.

I took a course in dressmaking, so I make clothes for myself and now for the grandchildren. I also took a course in interior design. I guess I want to know how to do everything from the inside out. I like to learn. See, if you develop an interest when you're young, then you'll have it for the rest of your life.

But the government makes it tough for older people. Taxes and the cost of living rise, yet our income stays the same. Why do you think I'm here aside from the fact I love the kids? The salary isn't much, but it helps.

A person who is lonely has to fight that problem. You must have will power. I have bouts of depression from time to time. Last Sunday it happened. So I'll talk to myself. I'll say, "What is this? Now get ahold of yourself. What are you, slipping? Do something!" So I'll bake, or I'll get on the sewing machine, or I'll jump to the piano.

There are an awful lot of people my age who are in wheelchairs, who are confined to institutions, who are dying. I think of them and know I have to be thankful and stop pitying myself.

MARJORIE CRAIG, physical fitness expert: I think women can be attractive for themselves and for men at any age. Just because a woman is sixty-five doesn't mean she can't be attractive. She can be as beautiful at twenty-five or forty. It's a different stage of beauty.

Marjorie Craig

PHYSICAL FITNESS EXPERT

Marjorie Craig is her own best advertisement for the exercises she has invented and adapted over a period of thirty-five years. At five feet, five inches tall, her weight a constant 115 pounds, she wears a size eight or ten, depending on the cut and quality of the outfit. And at sixty-seven she is living testimony that older age does not keep one from having a trim and healthy body.

Her first book, *Miss Craig's 21-Day Shape-Up Program,* was on the best-seller list for eight months. Another book, *Miss Craig's 10-Minute-a-Day Spot Reducing Program,* was published recently. Marjorie made visits to twenty-one cities to promote the book, demonstrating how to do these shorter toning and conditioning exercises.

For the past twenty-nine years she has been the supervisor and teacher of exercises at Elizabeth Arden's New York salon. The salon's red door is a Fifth Avenue landmark. The uniformed doorman welcomes me and holds the door for me. The elevator man tips his cap as I enter the off-white elevator with gray molding and a crystal chandelier. On the ninth floor a receptionist introduces me to Miss Craig.

She is blonde with blue eyes. Faultlessly made up, she wears a forest-green turtleneck leotard with black fishnet stockings and black high-heel shoes. She is slender with an enviable figure—especially her legs. As I follow her down the hall, conscious of my own imperfect posture, I stand up straighter.

Her office space is divided by a screen. On the near side are two couches, a glass cabinet with books and tape cassettes, an antique desk and two straight-back chairs. On the far side of the screen is a large mat covered with a pink sheet. There are stacks of pink towels and pink robes. A phonograph stands in one corner. "We always exercise to music," says Marjorie.

*J*ack and I have been married for forty-four years. I used to regret that we never had children, and I'd get very upset when I saw babies in carriages. But now it doesn't make any difference.

I met my Jack in college, when he was going with another girl. Then he and I both transferred to Columbia. I remember walking across the field to a football game with a girlfriend and seeing him with another man. I said to my girlfriend, "You take that one. I'll take Jack." And that was that. He's retired now, but he was in real estate.

We do everything together. We share household jobs. For example, I'll cook dinner and he'll do the dishes. Or I'll take care of breakfast and he'll check the pool—see if there are any frogs in the drain.

We like to go out to visit friends, have dinner. Friends will come to us, or we'll go dancing. But we're not the type to disco at Studio 54.

We also go on trips together. In May we were down in Rio, where I served as an exercise consultant to the Young President's Organization. They're all presidents of companies by the time they're forty years old. I think they have to have made three million dollars and have at least fifteen employees. They organize "educational weeks" for the members, with lectures during the day and parties every night.

I work hard and I love it. In fact, I'm sure that's what keeps me young.

Three times a year we go to Phoenix, Arizona, where I observe and work with the exercise teachers at the Maine Chance Farm. And the clients can have a class with me if they choose. Jack goes with me and it's a lot of fun.

I never go out without my husband and he never goes out without me. We're very close.

We had dogs for forty years; when one died we got another. They were members of the family. If they wanted to get on the sofa, they got on the sofa. If they wanted to get on the bed . . . We treated them as people. They thought they *were* people. If we were invited to a place where we couldn't take the dog, then we wouldn't go. We wouldn't put our dog in a kennel.

The last one died three years ago and . . . well . . . we just won't have any more. It hurt too much when something happened.

We live in Bedford, in Westchester County. I love to walk in the woods by my house. I try to relax, try to take everything in: the sky, the trees. I try to put things out of my mind and just enjoy the walk. I follow the deer paths, not the trails. The paths go up and down the terrain, up and down hills, and you can't always be sure where you're going to come out. But when Jack comes with me he marvels at my sense of direction.

When I was a child, I loved to work outdoors. After school I'd rake leaves, weed the garden, put wood in the woodshed. I didn't play with dolls too much. I loved to play ice hockey and football with the boys, and we'd have toboggan races.

I still love sports. I haven't played tennis in a long time, but I try to swim every day when I get home from work. My biggest hobby is painting. I love to paint: horses, animals or people. I can't paint still life.

My weekday routine goes something like this. I get up at six. I usually have a half grapefruit if they're in season, or an orange, my one slice of bread for the day and a cup of coffee. Then I drive to Mount Kisco for the train to the city. From door to door it's two hours. Four hours commute a day since 1950! I read on the train or play cards with some of the women.

Starting work at ten and ending at four, I give ten or eleven half-hour private classes a day. I work hard and I love it. In fact, I'm sure that's what keeps me young.

I hate the term "senior citizen." If human beings feel good, look good and can carry on their lives, why stick a name on them just because they're ten, twenty or thirty years older than they once were?

I've exercised all my life. With some of the exercise teachers here, I'm old enough to be their mother—but they get tired before I do. I don't feel older than them. I sometimes feel ageless.

I got my B.S. degree in physical education. Then I took

a postgraduate course in physical therapy at Columbia University Medical School. From there, I went to the Neurological Institute of the Columbia Presbyterian Medical Center and stayed for seven years. As a physical therapist, I worked with men, women and children who had damaged their muscles through accidents, or had lost temporary use of their muscles through illness or surgery.

When I was in medical school I cut up a cadaver. I took out every muscle, following each one to its origin. In a sense, that's the way I work out my exercises. I find out where the muscle is, where it starts and where it ends. I find out its function, and I make the exercises do what the muscle is supposed to do. Muscles are put there to be used in a certain way, and a good exercise program must take that into account.

I began working just with women in 1942. My classes consist of women of all ages. I have women in their seventies and young girls in their teens; some mothers even bring in their children (seven- and eight-year-olds) so that they can exercise together. These women come from all walks of life: doctors, teachers, housewives, lawyers, decorators. Years ago it was just society people. Now it seems every field is represented. Some women, who have been with me for over twenty years, have become friends.

I have some women in their sixties who do better than ones in their thirties. You can start exercising at any time of your life. When you begin you might have to take it slowly because your body isn't in condition, but once you learn the routines it's easy.

Someone might come in and say, "I want this spot reduced, this area trimmed," or, "I want to improve my posture." We work on it together. Over a period of time you *do* see results. The client will look better and feel better.

If women have physical infirmities, I can work out a program tailored just for them. No movements should be forced. The goal isn't pain; it's to have your body toned up and everything in good working order. If a woman has a physical problem like a bad back or arthritis, I ask for a note from her doctor.

A planned daily program is important in order to exercise every muscle in the body. Sports are good, like tennis and swimming, but when you participate in just one sport, you're really isolating certain movements.

Through exercise you can also improve your coordination, your flexibility and your posture. You can contour your figure all day long if you walk properly, sit properly and stand properly. According to the President's Committee on Physical Fitness, one of the ways to hold back the aging process—and deter the diseases that accompany old age—is exercise.

I have some criticism of the exercise shows that have been on television. An exercise with the woman lying on her stomach, raising her head and lifting her legs, ruins the back. Another done with a stiff leg, bending over, can also cause problems. I think exercise programs on television could be much better.

I don't recommend fad diets for any of my clients. If you are gaining weight, you're eating more food than your system needs. Your body can't take it, so you store it up in the form of fat. If you want to lose weight, you've got to cut the portions down. And don't eat sweets. The key is a well-balanced diet. I think your life should be balanced—like a seesaw. You should have a combination of proteins, carbohydrates, a certain amount of fats and minerals.

I tell my clients, "The only time you're enjoying that food is when it's in your mouth, where the taste buds are. When you swallow it, you aren't enjoying it." And there's an old saying by Dr. Harvey Kellogg: "You are what you put in your mouth, chew up and swallow. What you eat today is walking around and talking tomorrow."

Values are different from when I grew up. Today, mothers are letting their children grow up too quickly. As soon as a child is eleven, twelve, thirteen, they're going to parties, and their childhood is gone. Young girls dressed up in high heels are trying to behave like adults. I think a person should stay young and enjoy that time as long as possible. The responsibilities of an adult will come quickly enough.

I was always a responsible child, and I always obeyed my mother and father. When I was brought up you were supposed to respect older people, but that's not true today. I believe that everyone is born equal, and that everyone should be treated civilly and equally. I don't see why younger people and older people can't get along and respect each other.

I hate the term "senior citizen." Every time I hear it, it just ruffles my feathers. Why should we label human beings? If they feel good, look good and can carry on their lives, why stick a name on them just because they're ten, twenty or thirty years older than they once were?

Elizabeth Arden didn't retire me at sixty-five, and I'm sure I can continue here as long as I like. I don't believe in the mandatory retirement age. If a person is capable of doing the work the same way they did when they were younger, they should keep on working. If they fail in their work and they're not doing as good a job, that's something different.

I never think of my age until someone asks me how old I am. Otherwise I don't really think about getting older. Probably it's because I'm so involved with my work, with the people I come into contact with. I really think you're only as old as you feel. Expressions on a person's face can make them look older. If you feel sad and depressed, then the face and the body just sag and droop. Age isn't something to be depressed about. We all grow old. Accept the number and grow old gracefully—that's the way to do it. Be happy if you're sixty-five and healthy and well.

I think women can be attractive to themselves and to men at any age. Just because a woman is sixty-five doesn't mean she can't be attractive. She can be as beautiful as at twenty-five or forty; it's just a different stage of beauty.

I believe in God, but I don't feel that you have to demonstrate it. I think you find God within yourself.

I think you should keep your mind active. Read the papers every day. Listen to anything on television that's interesting—anything that has to do with politics, with what's going on in the world.

When I was a child, we didn't have Social Security or pensions. I was brought up to save my money for my old age, to have "sick money" to take care of an illness. Money is the best defense for old age so you don't have to be dependent on anyone. I'd want to be secure on my own.

I try to be a patient, kind, understanding person. People can hurt me, over and over and over again, and I'll take it—until, all of a sudden, I've *had* it. That's the end of our relationship. Maybe it's a weakness that I don't talk about it, that I don't confront the person.

Way back when I got married, they said it was a fifty-fifty compromise. But I sometimes think the woman gives ninety-five and the man gives the rest. A woman has to give in more because she's more understanding. A man probably thinks he gives just as much, but I don't think it's always true.

I was brought up with the idea that you don't have to go to church to be a good person. I believe in God, but I don't feel that you have to demonstrate it. I think you find God within yourself.

I don't feel bad about growing older. There's only one thing that bothers me: what would I do if I couldn't go on with my work? I love teaching, working with people, helping people accomplish what they want to accomplish.

I live for today, and I look forward to what I can do in the future with my work. At the moment, I'm satisfied.

Nellie Thompson

Nellie Thompson, seventy-eight, lives with her husband Earl in Broward County, Florida. Their house is cozily cluttered with handmade objects, stuffed animals and china knickknacks.

An American flag flies from a pole in their front yard, a duplicate to the one in the back. Nellie and Earl used to raise the flags only on holidays, but now they do it every day. Nellie says, "I'm proud to be an American. I think this is the best country in the world. I wish everyone would fly the flag as a positive symbol of belief."

Nellie is active in the Silver-Haired Legislature, a lobbying group for senior citizens of Florida. The "legislature" includes 38 senators and 119 representatives. Their work is funded by a $50,000 federal grant to give the elderly better access to state government.

Last year Nellie helped develop and pass a bill for community care. This provides funding for special projects such as Home-Touch, a communications outreach program. She also worked successfully to obtain state funds to contribute to the cost of dentures, eyeglasses and hearing aids for the elderly.

The lobbying issues on her agenda for 1980 include: required courses in geriatrics for medical students; tuition-free admission to state universities on a space-available basis; public health-care clinics for the elderly; and a ceiling imposed on costs of hospitals, doctors and drugs.

The Thompsons' house is one of twenty houses electronically monitored by the Council on Aging in Saint Petersburg. Under this model project, if Nellie or Earl falls ill, they can summon help immediately. They can press one of several buttons attached to their refrigerator, bathroom cabinet and lamps.

Nellie and I sit at the dining-room table. The North Fork of New River canal is visible through a wall of picture windows. The backyard is lush with greenery. During the interview a mango falls on the roof, the sound startling to me but commonplace to Nellie.

Her hair is white, her skin as translucent as porcelain. She wears glasses with light-colored frames. Her orange sleeveless dress has embroidery around the yoke.

*T*his is the second year that I have been elected to the Silver-Haired Legislature as a senator from Broward County. You need a hundred signatures just to get on the ballot. I will go to the state capital, Tallahassee, in July. Last year the seniors who attended were aged sixty to ninety-four, from all walks of life. Our hours, from the time we arose, were six in the morning until eleven or twelve midnight. This lasted for a week. Everyone was very alert and active.

The Florida Silver-Haired Legislature has been in existence for two years. We've patterned ourselves after the successful program in Missouri. We prepare our own bills, take them to Tallahassee and then use the Senate and

House chambers to do all our work in the Capitol. Then we turn our bills over to the real state representatives. I *know* the Silver-Haired Legislature works; we've had five bills pass through the Florida Senate.

When the person comes along that you're really interested in and really love, he's going to stand out and you won't even see anyone else.

One is a hospital-cost-containment bill. This will benefit not only the senior citizens, but everybody. With this bill you pay for just what you receive in the hospital. Each patient will receive an itemized statement of every test and treatment. A hospital can't pad its bills. A patient won't wind up having unnecessary procedures just to pay for some new machine.

My husband was in the hospital for three days, and his bill was over three thousand dollars. We're still getting bills from doctors we've never seen or heard of. So this has got to stop.

We're also interested in transportation. We're going to discuss it in Tallahassee this coming session. A lot of seniors don't have money for cabs. They don't have cars, and the bus service is terrible. They can't go shopping, they can't get to a doctor, and this is pitiful. We want vans or buses provided on a regular basis, on a scheduled route.

I'm also chairman of the blood bank of the Broward County Community Council. It's a volunteer job. Fifty senior-citizen clubs belong to the blood center—4,900 members. For fifty cents a year each member can have up to three pints of blood. Before we reorganized, we were buying blood. Now it's all donated. I keep all the paper-work of blood taken in and blood dispersed.

I was born on November 2, 1900, in a little Pennsylvania mining town called Marguerite, thirty miles east of Pittsburgh. My father was a stable boss for the H. C. Frick Coal & Coke Company. We lived in a company house. There were eleven of us: five boys, four girls and my parents. We had large gardens, so we had plenty to eat; and mother made a lot of our clothes.

My father took us to school when the weather was bad in a wire-wheeled buggy or in the sleigh. Otherwise, we walked the two miles back and forth. In those days, this was nothing unusual.

I don't believe there's any one person I have set up as a model to pattern after. But during my life it has been my practice to study people. From the time I was a little girl, I would watch the way people walked, in order that I would learn to walk gracefully. The same with speaking: try to have a soft, relaxing and interesting voice. These things I picked up by myself.

When I was fourteen years of age, I thought, "If I could only stay this age, it would be wonderful." At that time my sister had learned to sew, and she made me such beautiful clothes. I was a nice height, slender, and I wore my hair down my back in natural curls, a golden color. I had lots of friends. I didn't go with boys except to skating rinks with a crowd. There were many things I could do around the house to help my mother and I just enjoyed it. I always had time to play also. I still love to see girls in their teens. They're beautiful.

I don't believe in premarital sex. I really think when a young man marries a girl, he wants to think she is clean and pure, not trash.

I have been married four times. I was on Cloud Nine each time, and all four marriages were very happy. With my first husband I had my children, whom we loved dearly. We took care of his parents, who loved me as if I were their daughter. He died.

My second husband was retired, and we were so happy just doing things for each other. He expired also.

After six years, I married my third husband. He was so much like my second husband that it seemed that I just picked up where I had left off when my second husband died. They were childhood friends, grew up together and worked together. I had known him for twelve years. He was wonderful, but lived less than two years.

We were living in Florida then, having come from Detroit in 1955. After he was gone, life became very different. I didn't want to be a third or fifth wheel. I didn't want to run around with couples.

I joined the Michigan Club, a social club for people from the state of Michigan. There were an awful lot of widows. I took them places and organized things. They were reaching for something. There was a need. I was helping them but I was also helping myself. I had a lot of dinners and got to know a lot of people.

I met my present husband at the Michigan Club. Friends of mine introduced us. I was seventy-three at the time, and he was seventy. When the person comes along that you're really interested in and really love, he's going to stand out and you won't even *see* anyone else. Your thoughts will come right back to him. That's the way it's always happened to me. He'll stand out above everyone else. That's how you'll know you love him.

I'd rather be married than single. I don't like living alone. But if I had to be alone, I'd invite people in. I'd make my own amusement. I don't get lonesome because I crochet, I knit, I sew. I make many of my own clothes.

I'd never in my life ask a man to go out with me. I think the trouble with a lot of women down here is they're crazy for a man, and they try too hard to nail 'em. If you're not looking, you have a better chance.

Men like to feel important, and I think it's nice for women to let them know they *are* important. After they lose them, they find out how important men are.

I think it's fine for women to learn how to do everything, and I don't think it's a disgrace for women to do any kind of work. I've driven a tractor, milked cows, fed pigs. My first husband and I lived on his parents' farm until they died. We had our own restaurant for ten years. We had a gas station at one time, and I used to pump gas.

Now it's almost necessary for women to work, especially when everything is so expensive and where a family's involved. But I still think you can make the man feel he's the head of the house. Even if you know the answers to questions, you can still ask them. The man should be in charge. The woman shouldn't belittle him.

When I was first married on February 25, 1918, I knew very little about sex. My mother explained things to us girls, and my father did likewise to my brothers. But we never read about it or saw pictures like the children of today. It's embarrassing to walk into a drugstore or a bookstore and see young teens looking at these books. I've been working to get these stores to take them off the shelf.

I don't believe in premarital sex. I really think when a young man *marries* a girl, he wants to think she is clean and pure, not trash. For couples living together, I think they feel they have more freedom to walk away from each other if things don't work out. They may have children, then separate, and the children are the ones that suffer.

To me, marriage is a very serious thing. Marriage is something that two people must work at. You must learn to share things with each other, both happiness and grief. You must talk things over and make the right decisions. You must really love each other and do kind things for each other while you are both together.

*The aged can offer the younger generation
their knowledge and experience of things
that happened in the past. All the younger
generation need do is listen.*

I don't like divorces. But if two people are not suited for
each other and they are both very unhappy, then I think
it's better to be apart than living together and quarreling
all the time. If there are children, this is not a good environment for them either. It can have a very great effect on
them in later life.

The first time I felt old was when I got sick.

On my birthday, November 2, 1970, I was collecting
money for flowers for a neighbor who had died, when a
large dog bit me on the arm. I froze. I could not talk or
move. His master released the dog from my arm.

In just a week my third husband became ill, and I had to
take him to the hospital. He lived ten days. This was such a
shock to my system that I developed an inflammation of
muscles and nerves all over my body. I was taken into the
hospital, and the only thing that would help me was corti-
sone. I was completely paralyzed. When I could not walk
or feed myself, I really felt old. After the stay in the hospital, my two daughters took turns staying with me, a month
at a time, for four months. It took me a year and a half to
recover.

I feel real good now. I have pernicious anemia. I take
three iron pills a day, which I've prescribed for myself, and
one blood-pressure pill. Other than that, I just try to forget about my health. God's given me the grace and power
to *go* 'cause I'm busy as can be.

I think growing old is a God-given privilege. I'm lucky
to live this long, to have a sound mind, and still be physi-

cally able to take care of myself. So many people die young and never have that privilege. I believe that your body is precious and that you should take wonderful care of it. If you stop to think, your body functions better than any man-made machinery. Many people abuse their bodies and age very quickly.

I've never worked harder in my life than I'm doing now. I think that working at *anything* keeps you young. You can't quit. If you have an arm and don't move it, you lose it. The same with your brain. You've got to use your whole body—your eyes, your ears, your brain.

As a child, I was very interested in the piano. I started taking lessons twice. But each time, after I took lessons for several months, my sister became ill and we would be quarantined for a month. After that I studied by myself and was able to play the piano for entertainment and pleasure, for the Sunday school and church. I played for the church until I was thirty-three years of age. Then we bought our restaurant. With all the work and my children, I gave up the piano. Anything that you give up, you lose. So now I do not have a piano, and I have lost all that I ever knew about playing one.

We're up by 8:00 A.M. and usually asleep by 11:45. Earl has the radio going most of the day. The house is wired throughout. It could be turned to the news or to some soft music.

I think "Barnaby Jones" is our favorite television show. The characters and situations seem so lifelike. We also enjoy quiz shows. We like to guess along with the contestants.

I never have time heavy on my hands. Years ago I learned to sew, to make hats, to do needlepoint. I try to find time for crafts. But mostly I like to do things for other people. I find that it gives me a great amount of pleasure. On every special occasion, I prepare meals for a black couple who are shut-ins: Christmas, Thanksgiving, New Year's, birthdays, Mother's Day, Father's Day and Easter.

They are so pleased and very appreciative, and it makes me happy that I can do something for them. I have been doing this for three years.

I've had many friends during my life, at the various places I've lived, some of whom I've kept in touch with for many years. Right now my best friend is my sister-in-law. We've been friends for fifteen years. I introduced her to my husband's brother-in-law, and they were married five years ago. They were married on our first wedding anniversary so the four of us could celebrate together. On the sixteenth of every month, we put on long dresses and go to a fancy restaurant for dinner.

I don't believe there should be a mandatory retirement age. Many older people can do a better job than someone younger. When a person is disqualified due to their age, they feel it is the end for them. My father was discharged at seventy years, due to his age, and insurance would not cover him any longer. He thought the end of his life had come. At that time my brother gave him a job, and he worked for ten more years. My brother could not get anyone who could do the job as well as my father did.

You shouldn't leave funeral plans for your children to decide. My father would never talk about death. He died when he was eighty-five with no plans for a burial plot or anything. My sister and her husband finally took care of things. My mother was too old to handle that burden, and it really wasn't fair. Now we plan as much as we can while we're living. After you're dead, you're dead. It's too late for discussion.

With each one of my husbands, I made funeral arrangements. I have three places that I can be buried. The last time I married, Mr. Thompson and I discussed this matter before we were married.

After we were married, we went to the Lauderdale Memorial Gardens, and I made him acquainted with the people in the office. I told them that I did not want Mr. Thompson to have any trouble in case I expire first. I'll be buried in a crypt beside my second husband. Mr. Thompson will be buried beside his wife.

I never liked the thought of cremation. The price of regular funerals for my three husbands ranged from seven hundred dollars to fifteen hundred. Now I understand the price of a regular funeral is thirty-five hundred. The cremation runs four hundred dollars if you make arrangements now. If prices keep going up and I live many more years, I just might have to be cremated.

I've never worked harder in my life than I'm doing now. I think that working at anything keeps you young.

I believe in life after death. If you look at the trees, the flowers and the things that come up after they die, how could you believe anything else? You're told in the Bible that we're brought back. I don't believe I'd come back like I am right now. But I do believe in the hereafter. If you can take a little dead seed and plant it, and *that* comes back—well, God takes care of it.

If you have love and religion in your heart, it shines on other people whether you know it or not. I try to set a good example for people. Love, religion and charity seem to go together. I don't believe you can have one without the other.

God gives us the strength to carry any burden we might have, if we have faith in him. I really don't fear anything about growing old. So when I ask God to watch over me, I have faith that he will. I thank him each day. I live one day at a time and get the most enjoyment out of it. If there's anything bad, I just try to forget it. Many people worry about something that might happen the next day. But when the next day comes they make out somehow. So why worry?

Nothing really provokes me. I've worked with the public too long to take every little thing seriously. I don't like arguments or quarrels. I stay away from people who do. If someone's going to be a source of irritation I just ignore them. I consider the source and let what happens roll off my back.

I have always tried to live an honest, upright life so that my husband and children don't have to be ashamed of me, and my friends won't be happy I'm among the missing. I would like to be missed a little bit, because if you aren't missed, you don't amount to much.

I will be remembered for a long time. In 1976, I was the twenty-first person in the United States to be named to the Joe Kappler Senior Citizen Hall of Fame. My picture and a list of all the things I have done in the past fifteen years are in an album in the library in Everett, Washington, and my name is on the plaque hanging on the wall. In 1978 Mr. Thompson and I were two people out of six to receive the first Broward County Senior Citizens Hall of Fame award. Our names are on a plaque hanging in the Court House in Fort Lauderdale, Florida. In 1977 Mr. Thompson and I were selected Oakland Park, Florida, Senior Citizens of the year. Those things will be there long after I'm gone.

I'm very happy now. I feel I'm the most fortunate person in the world. I've had a happy, busy, productive life—good husbands, good children and stepchildren. Perhaps that's why I don't *feel* old. I am really blessed. I just hope we can be able to live as we are for many years.

The aged can offer the younger generation their knowledge and experience of things that happened in the past. All the younger generation need do is listen.

MARGUERITA RUDOLPH, author and educator: (with friend, opposite): I will plan my own festive funeral, with music, some original entertainment or performance, with a showing of slides of me in action and a recorded farewell.

MAGGIE KUHN, below, "Gray Panther": Some women are becoming radicalized in their old age. Perhaps they've divorced, or they find out they don't have a pension. When they conquer their traumas, they can really turn things around.

SHIRLEY POLYKOFF, above, advertising executive: My husband was a lawyer, and he believed in career women. I've always believed it takes twice as much energy to have a job, a husband and children. But you get twice as much back!

*MAXINE SULLIVAN, above, jazz
singer: The mandatory retirement
age is ridiculous. I can remember
when forty-five was supposed to be old.*

*KATHERINE HOBSON, sculptor: From the first day I took a sculpture lesson, I
knew that was what I wanted to do. I wrote my mother and said, "I'm not going to
Radcliffe. I'm going to study sculpture.*

Katherine Hobson

SCULPTOR

Katherine Thayer Hobson is a sculptor. She is ninety years old. At City Hall, in May 1979, the mayor presented her with a bouquet of roses and a birthday message for "a life filled with notable achievements." She serves on the board of directors of several art societies. Her prize-winning work has been exhibited in galleries and shows all over the world.

Our appointment is for one o'clock in the handsome old apartment house where she lives. I stand outside her door and ring the bell until twenty minutes past one. Have I misunderstood the day or the hour? I leave a note and go home.

Later that afternoon, Katherine calls to say she forgot to mention she is a little bit deaf. We set up a new meeting.

Upon entering her duplex apartment, I am startled to find myself in a working studio crammed full of statues. There are over thirty pieces—large and small. The blinds are drawn to cool off the room on this hot, muggy June day. I follow her small stooped form as she

shuffles slowly along in her black patent-leather flats.
We pass the completed busts of men, women, children—and horses. Three modeling stands are covered
with cloths, a sign of work in progress. There is dust everywhere. Old newspapers and magazines are stacked in
piles.

We walk through the living room, where the furniture
is old and worn, the upholstery faded by time into muted colors. We sit at the dining-room table, an electric
fan whirring behind us. Through the open window
comes the noise of traffic from the street four flights below.

Katherine, plump and gray-haired, sits primly in her
black-and-white dress. Her hands stretch out in front of
her on the table. There are moments when my voice
does not carry clearly enough. I repeat and rephrase my
questions, my voice rising in volume.

Katherine speaks with a breathy rhythm. Her eyes
twinkle. She laughs frequently and appears to be enjoying herself tremendously.

*E*ver since I can remember I've always wanted my
own way. I'm very domineering. I must have been
a very difficult child, a difficult sister.

As a child I was not interested in children's
things. When we played games in our family, we had to
play games out of mythology or the Bible or something
that had some meat to it. Play had a purpose to it.

Mother taught me to read at the age of four. She later
said it was the greatest mistake she'd ever made. From that
time on I was lost to the other children. Here was this
wonderful world of books, and everything seemed to be
inside it. I wanted to do nothing but read. But Mother said
that you could do it only two hours a day. I was very wick-
ed. I would lock myself in the bathroom where they
couldn't get me and say that I had diarrhea!

The result was that I had all this knowledge which the

average child doesn't have. That's one reason why I was so absolutely at home with adults.

An astrologer told me I'll probably die in a sudden accident. That's given me the most wonderful freedom! It's put me above all these little things that happen.

As a child I was very fond of sculpture. We had some small statues, a few little bronzes, around the house. At the age of seven I was in Boston having my portrait painted. My nurse, to amuse me in some spare time, took me to the Boston Museum. I came home and informed the family I was going to be a sculptor. I was never given any clay or Plasticine to work in. I used to paint and draw, the way all children do. I had paint boxes but I never had a chance to try to model.

My parents were people of great character. My father was a very independent person. His parents had lost everything in the Civil War. His mother was left a widow with small children with no money, on a plantation with no slaves. So she started a school for the children of her cousins and friends, which was apparently a great success.

My father graduated from the University of Virginia before he was twenty-one. He went West, young man, because there were greater opportunities out there. He was the youngest district attorney in Colorado. There were hard times. He was a stranger. But he was the kind of person who hung on—who did the thing he made up his mind to. I guess I got some of that from him.

My mother was a very gentle, lovely, feminine person. But she knew exactly what she wanted. When my father died while we were still quite young, she did everything she could to give us a well-rounded and varied education.

She took us all abroad after the deaths of my father and

her mother and her only brother. I was thirteen. We lived in Europe for three years. Then she said she wanted the boys to be American citizens. They'd have to be brought up in America. It was all very well that they'd had foreign languages and music and art and all that, but they were Americans and boys. So she left me in Germany and took them back to the States.

I lived in a pension with a very nice family and went to school in preparation for college. I was sixteen.

From the first day I took a sculpture lesson, I knew that was what I wanted to do. I wrote my mother and said: "I'm not going to Radcliffe. I'm going to study sculpture."

She was quite surprised. But she didn't worry about it until I sent her pictures of my first work, a nude lady. I named her Eve, since she was my first creation. Then I told my teacher I wanted to do a man; I wanted to do an Adam.

With simplicity in my heart I took a picture of him with my little Eastman Kodak and sent it to Mother. And Mother hit the ceiling! It was bad enough, she said, to make and know a woman, but a girl of sixteen to model a nude man! She just couldn't stand it.

I wept buckets of tears over her letter and wrote her a furious one back saying she'd insulted me and she'd insulted art. That nude man meant no more to me than . . . a chair!

She came right over to Germany to see me. She said, "Well, if you're really serious about this, then you're going to do it properly."

I couldn't go to a German art academy in those days. Women weren't allowed. We were in Dresden, a nice quiet city. There were opera and theater, everything cultured that you could want. It was a much quieter place than Berlin at the time.

So I studied privately, all arranged by Mother. In an academy, it's kind of a hit-and-miss thing. You may be observed by the professor but it's sporadic. You look at what other students are doing and perhaps you copy. You get away from your own true talent. So I got far more attention than I would have got in an academy.

In some ways I've found that often what seems like limitations have been to my advantage.

I came back to America in the summers. I studied my sculpture in the winters in Germany. Then I met a tall, blond young man, fell in love and got married.

When he proposed, I said, "I could never give up my sculpture."

And he said, "I never would have asked you to marry me if I thought you would." He was very broad-minded. It worked out pretty well. I always managed to work at home. I had either a big north room or a studio.

We got divorced after a while. I don't remember how many years—numbers mean nothing to me—and he married again. A very nice woman. He had two sons. They're nice boys. We get on very well.

I've lived this long, so I feel I can do anything I want. I eat all the things I shouldn't eat and enjoy them thoroughly.

I left Germany under Hitler. Hitler upset me very much. I later heard that all my letters to America were being opened and photostated. And I wasn't even political!

I went to Greece and met a charming young man whom I married. I was physically strong then. We had a wonderful time traveling by freighter, exploring the islands by muleback.

We came back to New York City and took a nice little apartment on the East Side. Unfortunately, my husband developed too much of an interest in other ladies. Well, you see, there was a great dearth of young men because of the war. All the young men went to the front, and here was this young man who wasn't subject to the military because he wasn't a citizen. I stood it for a while, and then I ended it. He married again, and now he too is dead.

For young artists to get ahead, I think it's important to have American teachers. It's all very nice to study in Europe, as I did, but the rewards just haven't been the same. You go to some school here, or to a man who has a lot of students. He knows you, he has friends, contacts. When there comes an exhibition you send something in and the jury says, "Oh that's so-and-so's little pupil." So it helps to be sponsored in a sense.

I've sculpted people, horses. What else is there? Horses because I love them and I've always ridden. Nowadays I love the races. I go to the track every Saturday—by bus, by myself. I look at the program very carefully. I've modeled some of the horses, and sometimes I go down to the paddock and look them over. I know very often what I want to bet on. It's not a very great sum of money.

I never had any children. I suppose I wouldn't have been as free. I've moved around quite a bit.

I'm very devoted to my nieces and nephews. We get on beautifully together. Sometimes I think I get on better with them than their parents do. For one thing, I have no real authority. If I interfere with them, they know it's because I'm fond of them and because I want them to appear in the best light always. It's a different relationship from the one you have with your mother.

I went through the First World War in Germany when we had almost nothing to eat. When I came back here to the island of New York, I realized we could be so easily cut off and I vowed never to be without food. So I started buying canned foods. Due to the vicissitudes of life, I thought they'd be useful if we had a storm or another blackout or if I were sick. Then, being a very busy person, I'd forget all about them.

I had a cabinet with three shelves, absolutely crammed

full. One morning last week, at about four, some of them just exploded. It was a mess. I thought this must be a judgment. But I have two other cabinets of recent purchases. If I see a nice can, I just can't resist.

My sister is horrified at the way I live. She came over and cleared away a whole lot of cans. The counters were a sticky mess, just glop all over the place. The cockroaches seemed to love it. My sister was quite disgusted by them. Well, they don't bite you. They don't sting you. They may startle you but they won't hurt you. They'd be rather admirable creatures—the rapidity with which they move—if they wouldn't reproduce so frequently. The cans were a symbol. You see, I always felt so safe, with cabinets nice and full. "Well," my sister said, "it's ridiculous."

I don't have anyone to help me. People who come in to clean seem so slow and they're all terribly expensive. I can do a lot with that money. I have a little cart that I take marketing.

I don't like polishing shoes or silver or mopping the floors. So I just don't do it. I used to be concerned about these things but I'm not any more.

I had a ganglion on my hand, like a knob, a big swelling. They tell me that they used to take a big heavy family Bible and smash it down on your hand and get rid of it that way. But that's not so good because the thing has roots and unless you get the roots out, it comes again. So I went into the hospital to have it taken out. That was a traumatic experience. My right hand, my working hand, was involved.

It was a beautiful operation. You can't see any scars. The surgeon is supposed to be *the* person for hands. I was conscious the whole time. I wanted to watch but they covered my hand with a sheet and I couldn't see.

I shared a room with three other women, and one seemed really crazy: a small dark wispy creature in a scarlet dressing gown who spoke no English. She spent her days and nights just pacing up and down. After the operation I woke up in my bed and that lady was standing over me. It was dark and she looked quite strange. I told her to please move, that I didn't like people watching me when I slept. She moved to the wall and began kissing it; perhaps she was kissing her shadow. Another patient went and got a nurse. The next morning that lady apologized to each of us in broken English.

I suddenly realized that the poor old thing was terribly afraid. Instead of being scared, I should have considered her—that she was in a strange place, with very little command of English, and that she was terrified. She was later moved to a private room. I really felt I had failed her. After all, what is life? It's rising to those challenges. It's putting yourself out.

In three weeks I was using my hand again.

A woman does not have complete equality in the art world. I just won't get those big commissions. So what should I do? Stop working? Never!

I'm interested in astrology. According to my Uranus and Sun being in a square, I'll probably die in a sudden accident. I went to an astrologer for confirmation. This was around fifty years ago. He said it would hit me so suddenly I wouldn't know what had happened. And, you know, that's given me the most wonderful freedom! I've never worried about anything since. It's like mental hypnosis. It's put me above all these little things that happen.

When I die, I'm going to leave everything I haven't sold to the Emma Willard School. My mother went there. Emma Willard was one of the first people interested in education for women. The school is a beautiful place outside Troy, New York.

I want to be buried because it's the natural course of nature. You are a part of the future fertilization of the earth. I'd rather do that, which is somewhat creative, I think, than be burned up.

I'd like some nice music at my funeral, perhaps something from Handel's *Messiah.* I guess I'd like someone to say that the things I valued the most in this world have been the people I've loved, art, music to some degree and poetry. You know, what people have meant to you is not always what you've meant to them. And it's very hard to realize how other people see you.

I have one friend who calls up and almost spoils my scrambled egg every morning. She calls from her office so it doesn't cost her anything. At first it irritated me no end. How dare she check up on me! But now I appreciate it. My niece said, "She only does it because she loves you so." And I thought, "Well, this is a lesson to me, and in the future I must be more gracious."

I believe in the hereafter and I believe in ghosts. I had curious experiences as a child. My sister and I would go to sleep and I'd be sure that dear grandma would be up and about, standing by the washstand. Well, I'd fall asleep and my sister would stay up trembling. At the time I thought, "Well, I don't mind seeing them. But if they touch me, I'll die."

I'd crawl under the sheets, pulling them up to my eyebrows. Then I decided this was a weakness. Each night I'd pull the sheet down a little more; to my nose, to my chin, to my shoulders. Then I'd stick an arm out. So I cured myself.

Now I don't think I'm afraid of anything. With all the crime around, it doesn't occur to me that somebody might hurt me.

I get up any time from six on, depending when I feel like it. I have two different rhythms. Sometimes I take a bath right away and then get dressed and have breakfast. Or I'll put on a wrapper, have breakfast first, dust a bit, then take my bath and get dressed.

Yesterday I was very lazy. I'm quite ashamed of myself. On Saturday, I had quite an exhausting day at the track, so I didn't do anything on Sunday. I just watched television. Shocking! I had such a bad conscience about that.

Anyway, then I generally make up my bed. By that time it's supposed to have aired. If I don't feel like doing that, I just let it air a little longer! Then I generally work.

In the winter I go to a lot of meetings. I belong to a lot of societies. I have dinner out with friends. At the end of the day I'll have a cocktail or a glass of wine. I've lived this long, so I feel I can do anything I want. I don't worry about my diet. I eat all the things I shouldn't eat and enjoy them thoroughly.

I like to cook. It can be quite creative. My brother once said my ambition was to use every pot in the kitchen and make every recipe in the book. Now I'm not as fussy because I have too much to do. At that earlier time I didn't have so many meetings or pupils or sculpture commissions.

I go to sleep whenever I'm tired. If I've had a very long day and been on my feet a lot, I may even go to bed at eight-thirty or nine o'clock. If something comes up, of course I'll stay awake. My idea is to have seven or eight hours of sleep a night.

I have a theory that in sleep you renew your contact with the earth. You get all your fresh strength from the earth. In fact, in the summer, if I'm in the country I like to lie down right on the ground, in the sun. I try to absorb the earth and the sun together.

Oscar Wilde was quite right when he said, "The tragedy is not that one grows old, but that one remains young." I'm quite a romantic. I've had every kind of romantic relationship with people I don't know at all. It's just imagined. You have all the thrill of the thing without the disillusionment of reality. I find that something you think about beforehand and plan is apt to be disillusioning when it comes. It's the surprising things in life which are the really thrilling things.

That's one of the problems with marriage. A young girl thinks about marriage, plans for it, thinks it's going to be all heavenly and perfectly wonderful. Somebody will love her so much; she will love him so much; they're going to be happy forever after. Then she marries that person and discovers he's very nice but he's quite human. And she can't help but be disappointed.

I think it's a good thing in marriage when two people are physically suited to each other. But that's not the most important thing. There should be a similarity in taste. If possible they should work together in some way. In one of my marriages I was able to translate my husband's books from German into English. I think it's a great thing if you have some interest in common. A community of interests will keep friends together for a lifetime.

I feel I've been completely liberated. I've always shared all kinds of work and responsibilities. I approve of a woman doing anything she can do well. You have to make choices and weigh values. Yet the reality is that a woman does not have complete equality in the art world. I've realized that. I just won't get those big commissions. So what should I do? Stop working? Never!

There's no excuse for older people to be lonely, depressed or bored. My advice to them would be: Go and do! Get busy. If you can't produce, learn something.

I think raising a family is a very serious thing. It's a great responsibility when you realize you have some of the next generation in your hands to mold. Recently I told a great-niece, "My dear, if you have a child and bring that child up to be a fine citizen, you're doing a much better job than I'm doing by making a statue. After all, when I'm finished with a statue, it's just there. It's dead. But *you're* modeling a human being."

I've just lived to be ninety and have gone through a whole lot to reach a point of spiritual calm. I'm strong for my age. I'm not going to worry about the natural developments. I'm losing some of my hair. It used to be so long I could sit on it. I expect when it all falls out I'll wear a wig. If you worry about these things you just spoil your humor.

It's interesting to see how people's bodies change as they grow older, especially for a sculptor. For instance, have you ever realized that most men after they pass thirty look as if they're pregnant? They get these fat tummies. On a man one never looks on it as such. If it's a woman, they say, "Well, she must be expecting a baby."

As you grow older your insides sink a little bit. You're only supported by these two legs, so you droop. But why not just accept these things as part of natural fate?

I resent young people being rude to old people. I was brought up to show respect for the elderly. I had a wonderful time with the old people in my family, and with the mothers of my friends. They knew so much that was interesting. They could tell me so much that could add to my life.

I believe there's a hierarchy in life. Only when you get older do you really learn about life. You have to live a certain length of time and see people succeed and fail to know why they fail. That's valuable experience.

As long as people are able they should keep their jobs. Luckily I can't be retired from mine.

I realize that as I grow older I'll probably get less and less enthusiastic about sculpture because I have to stand when I work. That's one reason why I took up poetry.

I've written little verses since I was a small child. A few years ago I realized I'd need some quiet endeavor. Now I belong to three poetry groups. The work is very emotional for me. I write in the kitchen, late at night, when I'm tired. That seems to be the best time. Words will come to me without my thinking.

I think it's good for people to have more than one interest, more than one career. Several years from now I may not want to do any more modeling. At least if my brain were intact, I'd have my writing. I can't imagine myself with nothing to do. I have a desire to express what I feel.

I watch television very rarely. Till a year ago I never had one in the house. I'll turn on the radio in the morning when I'm getting dressed to find out who's been murdered in the night—comfortable little things like that!

I like to read, but I don't have enough time to do it properly. I guess I'll have to live a few more lives to get through all the important literature.

I used to go to bed when I was half-grown and ask myself, "Now what have you done today which will have some lasting importance?" It's been my feeling that I'm only here for a temporary time. So it's my duty to really accomplish something while I can. Yet I don't know if I have.

I think my strength came from my family. They were strong-willed, out to fight. If a thing was not quite right, not quite just, then we were ready to challenge it. We were very conscious of having a mission in life.

People should regard life as a school—to grow each day. We take so much for granted. Maybe we've had too much. We've had an abundance of food, clothes, housing, travel. And I think we haven't appreciated those things when we've had them.

There's no excuse for older people to be lonely, depressed or bored. My advice to them would be: Go and do! Get busy. If you can't produce, learn something.

Martha Heritage

Martha Heritage lives with her husband, John, in a fifty-foot mobile home in a trailer camp in Broward County, Florida. A smaller trailer, the one they call the "baby," is parked a few feet away. This is the one they hitch to their car when they go camping.

At sixty-five Martha is a tall, spare, athletic-looking woman—someone comfortable with the outdoors and hard work. She is dressed in khaki Bermuda shorts and a yellow-flowered sleeveless blouse. Her limbs are tanned, her short hair brown, her eyes hazel.

She proudly shows me around her ten-foot-wide home: the full kitchen with its dining table; the living room with a couch, two easy chairs and a sewing corner; the bathroom with its stall shower; and the bedroom large enough to accommodate a king-size bed.

The sun filters through the jalousied windows as birds provide background music to our conversation. We sip our coffee, enjoying the light breeze on this ninety-degree day.

John, recovering from eye surgery, listens in on our

conversation, frequently adding thoughts of his own. I can almost *feel* the bond between these two people. When Martha leaves the room for a minute, John tells me, "I was married twice before, and it was pretty rough. Well, now I've got a good woman, and I appreciate her."

Martha frequently hesitates before answering my questions. Her eyes look up from her hands folded in her lap. She glances at John. When she speaks, her tone is low-keyed.

For most of the last thirty years I've lived in trailers. In the beginning it was a convenience. At that time I was married to a yacht captain, and the owners didn't want us on the boat when they used it. When they left the boat, we'd go back and take care of it. We'd move it from place to place, wherever they wanted to spend the weekend. The boat went south in the winter and north in the summer.

So we had to have either a lot of apartments or a mobile home, something that we could move into while the owners were on the boat. The first trailer was a thirty-six-foot one, and I'd haul it back and forth by myself.

I met John at a square dance held in a trailer camp. This was in 1957. I had been in a head-on collision and had broken my arms on the steering wheel. With all the plaster on me, I looked like a mess. But he liked me anyway.

I wouldn't want to live in an apartment or in a house, where I'll bet you couldn't hear that bird squawking right now! In apartment houses, you very rarely get to know everyone. Mobile living is neighborly. And if you want to be left alone, you can be left alone. We just pull that curtain over the big door, and no one will bother us. But when you walk out, if there's anyone around, you know someone's going to speak to you. We know everyone here. They don't bother us; we don't bother them. But if there's a problem we'll help each other out.

*We celebrate our anniversary 365 days a
year. We don't give each other gifts just
on Christmas. I don't wait for occasions to
buy him something.*

Whenever we want to go somewhere, we just pack up
the small trailer, the baby one out there, and go. We love
the outdoors. We go camping a lot. That's another phase
of mobile living. The people you meet camping are tremendous. I don't think you can find a finer cross section of
people anywhere except in square-dancing.

The rules for the trailer park are usually made by the
owners of the park. They start out with a set of rules. As
different things happen, they may add some or take the
ones away that aren't applicable. It works out very nicely.
For instance, we have a rule here about no pets. A few
people have pets, that's true. But they really shouldn't be
in a trailer. They can be annoying to someone else. And
you wouldn't want to go off and leave them. That wouldn't
seem just.

If someone's interested in buying a mobile home, the
first thing to do is choose the area where you'd like to live.
Find a park that appeals to you. You can buy a trailer new
from a dealer, or secondhand from someone who's selling
out. Payment for space in a park varies. We pay $75 a
month, but we have a friend who pays $135.

John's mother used to live in a trailer right across from
us until she passed away two years ago. Some said it was
silly having two big trailers—the extra cost. But it was
worth it, for all of us. The privacy was important. It really
worked. If Mom came over here and got on our nerves,
we'd tell her to go home. And if we were in her trailer and
bothered her, she'd say the same. John's always said that
two women could never live under the same roof at the
same time, even if it was a mansion of twenty-five rooms.

My parents never interfered with my way of life. And I've always thought that people have a right to their own privacy, whether they're your parents, your children, your friends or your neighbors.

I have two children and eight grandchildren, one of whom is from Vietnam. I've had disappointments with my children. But when they go off on their own, it's their life. Of course, you wish they'd do so and so, or not do such and such. But what can you do?

The man who bought Mom's trailer, our next-door neighbor, was in the Sunday-school class I taught when he was nine! He's going to be married soon. It's nice having him around, seeing him all grown-up.

The grandchildren of the other trailer owners are fun. It's good to hear them carrying on, laughing and playing. They're life. Yet there's a hard-and-fast rule in this trailer park that after eleven o'clock there's absolute quiet. Everyone obeys it. But what kind of a world would it be without children around?

I think you have to be faithful. The sexual revolution is not for me.

I wanted to be a nurse when I grew up. But by the time I was ready to enter nursing school the educational requirements went from two years of high school to two years of college. I was too poor to get more schooling. I had to go out to work.

I've done a little bit of everything off and on. I did bookkeeping. I worked in a sewing store for quite a while. I sew all my own clothes. I've bought just one dress in twenty years—and that was an emergency, when we were out, and I was wearing shorts. To go to a certain restaurant with some friends, I had to have a dress to wear. So we bought one.

I make my slacks, cushions, curtains—why, everything around here. I like to sew. I learned when I was a member of the 4-H Club. You start off with a potholder, then you make an apron, then a little top. If you're interested you go on—and I did. I'll never forget my first dress. It was black with gray trim and I pleated the skirt. I was so proud of that dress! Sewing has become a great hobby with me. I love it. I'll let the rest of the place go if I have something interesting to make.

Being active keeps me young. I like to swim. I ride my bicycle almost every day. I've got a folding bike for when we go camping.

John and I have been together over twenty years. They've been wonderful. Not only do I love him, but first, last and always he's been my good, true friend. I married a youngster. He's six years younger.

I think, if you want a marriage to last, you've got to talk to each other. You've got to share the good and the bad.

John had a hemorrhage in his eye. He's had laser-beam surgery. For the time being, he has to rest. He's only allowed up one hour a day. He sleeps on that lounger chair for the time being. So far his vision hasn't been affected.

When I go to the doctor with John, the doctor lets me see what's happening. He puts a little extra mirror on, and I can see what the doctor's seeing. I saw the red spot from the beginning. Now it's breaking up, moving around, sort of darkish. I can tell it's getting out of the area. We're keeping our fingers crossed that he doesn't need more surgery.

We celebrate our anniversary 365 days a year. We don't give each other gifts just on Christmas. I don't wait for occasions to buy him something.

I think you have to be faithful. The sexual revolution is not for me. Young people are testing all the time. I think some day they'll regret it.

The Depression of the thirties, the deprivation—you were lucky if you had one pair of shoes. We grew up vowing to give everything to our children. And now a lot of those kids don't know what it's like to work. And they don't know what it's like to have to do without, to go hungry, not to have the necessities, much less the luxuries. If it happened all over again they wouldn't be able to cope. It would be disastrous. And we made it this way for them.

Older people don't have to blend in with younger people, just be friendly with them. There's so much to learn from all ages. We visited a disco owned by one of John's clients. You walk in—and that music just takes over! You can feel it vibrating through your system. When you're there, it just becomes a part of you. It's really fantastic. I'm glad that we went. It's better that the young people are there enjoying themselves, instead of out robbing gas stations.

My husband thinks I'm liberated. I like being a mother, a housewife, and so forth. But I know there are women who like to be in the business world. They're capable, and if that's what they want that's wonderful. Now we can choose what we want to do. If the woman has a better income or more ability, and the man takes over the house— why, I think that's wonderful. John and I used to take care of this park together: made the repairs, kept the grounds up, worked side by side.

Loneliness is caused by staying too close to oneself, worrying about oneself. If only we would worry about someone else!

It's the three of us—my husband, myself and the Lord. I really don't remember being depressed. And my grief I take to the Lord in prayer and find solace. We are faithful churchgoers. We believe in our religion.

We both want to be cremated. He'll be laid out in his volunteer-fire-department shirt. I'll probably be in a square-dance outfit. Ashes to ashes, dust to dust, going back to where you came from: I'd like my ashes to go in the ocean. To me, death is the spirit going out of the body, so therefore it's nothing you can really explain. I'd hope people would remember me as being a friend.

I have more or less enjoyed my whole life. I have no desire to be other than what the Lord wishes for me from day to day.

When you can help someone, you don't hurt so much yourself. People have to reach out, to find a friend. No matter what the circumstances, you can always find someone else to give to, even if it's just a kind word. Loneliness is caused by staying too close to oneself, worrying about oneself. If only we would worry about someone else!

I think what scares most older people now is the way the prices are rising. Every time you go to the grocery store, the prices keep getting higher and higher. And our incomes don't keep going up like that.

John and I save pretty good money on our freezer plan. We eat a lot better than if we had to go to the store each night. When we feel like eating steak, we just go outside to the freezer and get one. We also have frozen vegetables and fruits.

We bought the freezer and the first load of food by paying a fixed sum each month. We got the freezer paid for and we finished paying for the food in four months. The food has always lasted us at least six months. It's worked out very well. In a way it's a type of budgeting. Now maybe we go to the grocery store about once every other week for bread, salt, soap—that sort of stuff.

There's something wrong with our country when old folks have to steal food out of the markets to live. Who gives a darn about the sex life of a whale? Yet I read in the newspapers that that project cost one hundred thousand dollars. Well, the government should give that money to the people who need it!

I think people shouldn't be forced to retire. There are a

lot of people who've worked all their lives and they just don't know how to be unemployed. You hear of people who get retired and then live less than a year. People should have a hobby, some interest to get them up in the morning. Everybody needs activities.

Seeing trees, sunsets, enjoying the way things are now— that's camping. I love to fish whether or not I catch anything. I can just sit quietly on a bank for hours.

If everything were possible, I'd like to investigate this United States—hook the car to the trailer and go. There's so much of it that I'd like to see and know about. I've seen pictures, but it isn't quite like going and seeing it for yourself.

There's nothing you can do about getting older. You've just got to accept it.

The term "senior citizen" doesn't bother me. It's beautiful. You can go to the drugstore, say you're a senior citizen and get ten percent off on your prescriptions!

A few months later I receive a short, cheerful note from Martha: "John finally had to have the operation on his eye. He is fine and came out of it with 20/20 vision." I think of the afternoon we spent together and hope they'll be off camping in the not-too-distant future.

Shirley Polykoff

Shirley Polykoff's hair color has been reported in the press as a "discreet mixture" of Clairol's Fresh Honey and Innocent Ivory. It was she who brought Clairol products to prominence with such slogans as these:

> *If I've only one life . . . let me live it as a blonde!*
>
> *Does she . . . or doesn't she?*
>
> *Is it true . . . blondes have more fun?*
>
> *The closer he gets . . . the better you look!*

For many years she was the highest-paid employee, male or female, in what was then the seventh largest advertising agency in the world. She's earned a place in the Advertising Hall of Fame. She is author of the book *Does She . . . Or Doesn't She? and How She Did It.* After achieving financial success and a certain celebrity status in the business world, she "retired" to become president of her own company.

On the eleventh floor of an office building on prestigious Fifty-seventh Street, I step off the elevator. Facing me is a three-foot-long neon sign proclaiming SHIRLEY POLYKOFF. "Now, that's pizzazz," I say to myself.

Her advertising agency occupies the entire floor. She has a staff of thirteen. There are two full walls of honorary plaques, awards and certificates. Being named National Advertising Woman of the Year was, she says, "a highlight of my career. I felt that at last I'd been recognized—that I'd done it."

The furniture is blonde wood—of course! There are palm trees and fresh flowers. Behind her desk is a wall-to-wall counter stacked with projects in various degrees of completion. There are piles of file folders, papers and looseleaf notebooks.

Shirley is an attractive woman, now tan from the summer sun. She is five feet, five and a half inches tall and constantly watching her weight. She wears a wine-colored pants suit with a matching striped blouse. Her jewelry is large, heavy and gold. She declines to reveal her exact age. From her appearance I am unable to guess.

Shirley exudes warmth. She immediately puts me at ease. Her voice is soft and rich.

My mother had wanted a boy. I was the second of three daughters. My parents had already chosen the name Leo. A boy could be anything—most importantly, he could be a money earner—while a girl could only grow up to be a mother. Well, I was determined to be both, and to do it better than other people.

My parents were immigrants. They came here with a dowry: a straw satchel containing a feather bed, two pillows, one heavy Russian silver spoon and some dried fish. My father's first job in America was in a lumberyard. Then he sold ties for a while. He did a variety of things.

I grew up in a walk-up tenement in the Jewish section of Brooklyn. Then we moved to an Irish neighborhood. In search of upward mobility, we went next to Flatbush. Early on, my sisters and I were taught the value of school. Education was highly respected by our parents. Every day we went to the library. It was the only acceptable excuse for coming home late.

Money was tight with us. But my parents were always optimistic, always able to make jokes despite what seemed like impending financial disaster.

My mother was a pretty, gay woman. She loved parties. We always had a houseful of company. She used to sing Russian folk songs. And she was a wonderful cook. She made all our clothes from her own patterns. It was said she had "golden hands."

It takes twice as much energy to have a job, a husband and children. But you get twice as much back!

My mother had no formal education. But she taught herself to read and write in Russian and Yiddish. When she came here, she went to night school to learn English. She was a very capable woman. She can be proud: all her kids turned out fine. If I considered anyone to be my role model, it would be my mother.

We were brought up not to be religious but to know all the history that went into being Jewish. We were taught respect for ourselves in a world where there wasn't too much leniency toward Jews.

On Saturdays, when I was eleven, I sold women's coats in the basement of a Brooklyn department store. When I was fifteen, I went to work at *Harper's Bazaar* as a secretary. One day I got a call from *Cosmopolitan* for some quick copy for an ad that *Harper's* was planning to run. It was a pre-holiday weekend. No one was around. So I seized the opportunity, jumped in and wrote it. Well, disaster! I had spelled a number of important names wrong. Someone had to take the blame, and it was me. I was fired.

In the mid-twenties I experienced my first instance of discrimination. I was turned down as a file clerk, not because I was female, but because I was Jewish. At the next job interview, for a secretary's position, I gave my name as Shirley Miller, my religion as Christian Science. I got the job. I also felt tremendous guilt the entire time I was there.

I became a copywriter for a women's store in Brooklyn. Four bachelor brothers ran the store, and they were mad for blondes. This was before the minimum wage, and I was happy to take home nineteen dollars a week. By the end of the year I was earning eighty-five. At the same time I was going to New York University to earn my degree. During the day I worked. At night I went to school. It took me six years.

I met my husband, George, during the early days of the Depression. He used to see me regularly, having lunch with six or eight men. At the time, a woman copywriter was rare. George and I met by chance at a New Year's Eve party. I was going with two other men at the time. I remember saying to a friend, "Let's put another scalp on the belt." George thought that I thought I was pretty special. He considered me a challenge. I never knew any of this until after we were married.

I was Shirley Polykoff in the office and Polly (short for Polykoff) Halperin at home.

There were numerous jobs during those early years. Then I took some time off. For a while I settled into being the perfect housewife and mother. But I didn't know how to act as a lady in retirement. I tried to be a good homemaker. But I found I had too much energy and time on my hands. George didn't like me in this new role. And I didn't like myself either. So it was back to work.

In 1955 I went to Foote, Cone & Belding, the advertising agency. And my personal business success really began when the Clairol account was tossed in my lap by the copy chief.

My ad—the famous "Does she . . . or doesn't she?"— was in the works for probably my whole life. I was the middle child sandwiched between two beautiful brunette sisters. I was a blonde like my mother. When my hair began to darken I began the visits to Mr. Nicholas, a beautician.

When my husband died I lost my partner in bed, on the tennis court, on the ski slope, at dinner, the theater, movies. Thank God, I had my job.

In 1955 women who "colored" their hair were considered "fast." Women would never admit they *dyed* their hair. We had to overcome that, and the fact that women were fearful of their family's disapproval. So I knew we'd have to stress naturalness and a feeling of respectability.

I think of myself as the mass consumer. I sell a product first to myself. I've got to be able to identify with it. If I had a guiding principle for thinking through ad campaigns it would probably be: "Think it out square, then say it with flair!"

I felt very guilty going to business at that time. I felt guilty toward my husband because to most people it seemed that he wasn't successful enough. I felt guilty about our two daughters. So whenever there was a parents' event, I was always there the earliest and stayed the longest. In my mind, I was always busy "making up."

I had it better than most women. Since I made so much money I could afford to have a maid and a nurse. The maid was to take care of things like food, so my family didn't have to wait to eat just because I was working. And the nurse was to make sure that the children were not neglected in any way.

Today, when most women go to work, they have no place to leave their children. That to me is one of the really great heartbreaks of being a working mother. Let's say you have a divorced working mother who didn't get a big chunk of money. She has two small children. Well, she goes to work, and she has fears about the children's security. And she's stuck home at night. Baby-sitters are expensive. At this point, unless she's moving very rapidly on her job, she's in a no-win position.

I think the women's movement is terrific. I just think the transition is tough. At this moment I think women are worse off than they were before. I know it will be better.

I'm an earnest advocate of universal day-care centers with qualified and conscientious personnel. All women who want to work should work—and have peace of mind.

My husband was a lawyer. He believed in career women. He was always terribly supportive. That kind of caring made things a lot easier. I've always believed it takes twice as much energy to have a job, a husband and children. But you get twice as much back!

We shared twenty-seven good years before he died from cancer. He suffered for two years. He just got thinner and thinner. He looked like someone from the Dachau concentration camp. There was nothing anyone could do. When he died I lost my partner in bed, on the tennis court, on the ski slope, at dinner, the theater, movies. Thank God, I had my job.

My husband's dead almost twenty years. I never found anyone else I'd want to be married to. I've gone with several men for several years. When I say, "I don't want to get married," I lose them. Now I don't even have that choice.

Sex is fine, no matter what your age, if *you can find a partner. I don't take sex lightly. I have to know a man and really care about him.*

It seems to me that there's a tremendous shortage of eligible men. I'm glad to be my age. I'm sorry for the younger people when I look around. I'm sorry that women have to make such a fuss over available men. The men, meanwhile, are sitting there being so terribly spoiled. And some of them are not even that attractive.

Sex is fine, no matter what your age, *if* you can find a partner. I don't take sex lightly. I have to know someone and really care about him.

I'm a grandmother four times. One of my daughters works here. That's nice. I get to see her every day.

And I frequently see my other daughter and her family. They live, unfortunately, twenty miles from the nuclear plant at Three Mile Island. That radiation scare really worried me. I try to get out there, or they come to see me. We talk on the phone all the time.

I think the best way to get along with your children is to keep yourself from criticizing everything they do. I think it's habitual with mothers. We remember they've been our babies—so we're still straightening their dresses. If they say, "How do you like the way I hung that picture?" instead of saying, "It's terrific," we usually say, "I think it's a little crooked."

At least I used to say that. Now I desperately try to say and be more positive in manner—to think it out, before I say something which is a criticism. I believe our children are sensitive to whatever we say. I think, though, that it works both ways. Since I'm aware of that, I don't chastise myself too often. And they think I'm wonderful. It works.

I get up at seven, seven-fifteen. I do ten to twelve minutes of setting-up exercises every morning. It's the only thing that gets me moving. Unless there's an early meeting I'll be in the office at nine, nine-thirty. I have a car and driver to take me to work.

I try to have my hair done twice a week. For me, it's important. It's one of the lines I use in advertising. "If you catch yourself unawares in the mirror, you have to like what you see." I'd rather say that than, "Oh, my God! Is that me?" Anybody should do whatever makes them comfortable—face lifts, the works. If this is important to you, and you can afford it, then *do* it!

I try not to go out to lunch because that puts the weight on. While you're being very social with your client, you're eating bread and having drinks. I just don't need it.

I work until five, five-thirty. On my way home I'll stop at least three times a week to see my mother. She's ninety-seven and in a nursing home. That's extremely difficult. I never know what I'm going to find. She's in possession of her senses. It just takes longer for her to say something. It really pains me to see her. The older people around her seem so unattractive. It's frightening to me.

I haven't been able to face what I would like for me—except not to linger long. I don't know what one can do about old age, except not to let it interfere with your life. I don't have any answers, any solutions.

You're not lonely when you have art all around you. I enjoy coming home. It's like having friends to welcome me.

I'm crazy about fine art. I like composition and color. Or maybe it started because I always heard that copywriters hated art directors. I felt I had to be more broad-minded than that! I'm very active on behalf of the Whitney Museum and the Metropolitan. I go to a lot of social functions.

I collect, look at and enjoy art. I have a pretty good collection of stuff in my house. If someone wants to begin collecting, my advice would be to go around and *look.* To look and look and look—this educates the eye. And you get to know what you like. Join museums, read art books and look. I did. The director of the Museum of Modern Art has said, "To look at things, even bad things, is educational." This way, you learn.

I started out by just liking Impressionists. Then I moved to liking Byzantine art, then the Dutch masters. You're not lonely when you have art all around you. I enjoy coming home. It's like having friends to welcome me.

Every Saturday I go to the art galleries with my best friend, who is an artist. We'll leave at one, be back at six. We're walking all the time. Walking makes me feel good. We never let anything interfere with our Saturdays. It's our routine.

Everybody gets lonely, even when they're married. But you mustn't complain. You've got to get up and get out. You've got to do!

I feel old when I creak. Suddenly there's an arthritic pain in the back of my ear that scares the bejesus out of me. Or I'm sitting in one position and I can't unbend. When I look closely in a large mirror and see those wrinkles starting, I know I'm getting older.

But there's so much going on today that I'm glad I'm the age I am. Sometimes I think, "Gee, if I was only this smart ten years ago!"

I'm bothered by the amount of violence in our society. And I'm concerned the way the scientific experiments are going. I don't want a friendly clone living on my block. I don't think I want to be around even to see how that's going to turn out. I've lived through a very exciting span—automobiles, electricity and airplanes. I don't have any desire to fly to Saturn.

I think I'm a very dependable person. If I say I'll do something, I do it. I have common sense. I also think I try to start out by liking other people. I'm just lately learning how to say, "No," without pain.

I love to read, from the trashiest books to the best. I get tremendous satisfaction from the way some writers put words together. Joan Didion is a master at that, though she seems to me a most melancholy person. There's no time here to be melancholy, or to slow down. I love my work.

Yet I was a casualty of forced retirement. I was never feeling better, physically and mentally. Yet I was still due to be put out to pasture in February 1973. Foote, Cone & Belding tried to come up with some way I could stay on with sufficient independent status to exclude me from the mandatory retirement policy. Perhaps I could do special campaigns.

There was an idea here, I thought. I'd received quite a number of offers. Perhaps I could even open my own company! It was a frightening idea. I was scared and vulnerable after being protected for so long, knowing there was a whole agency, a large organization, behind me.

But here I am, in business for myself. We're doing well and our staff keeps expanding.

When I'm asked how to break into advertising, my advice is always the same. You've got to have something more to offer than a bachelor's degree and good intentions. You should make a portfolio of your own work. Take ads you don't like and rewrite them so you do. Your best strategy would be to begin with a small agency where you're forced to do a little of everything. The experience will prove invaluable.

I like what I've made of my life. I'm grateful. As I've always told my children, "Take the time to be aware that you're happy when you're happy. Don't wait till tomorrow to realize how happy you could have been yesterday."

Estelle Wolf

FRIEND OF CENTRAL PARK

I've been hearing about Estelle Wolf for months. She is said to be "old, active and not afraid to speak her mind." A friend of mine, interested in conservation, returns from a walking tour of a park, a garden or an historic mansion, raving about the energy and stamina of this woman.

The organization that sponsors the tours is the Friends of Central Park. And the hard-working woman who is responsible for mailings and for membership is ninety-four-year-old Estelle Wolf.

When I call to set up a meeting, her voice on the telephone is clear and strong. She is going out of town; if we're to meet, she explains firmly, I must visit her *soon.*

Estelle lives in a one-bedroom apartment on the Upper East Side of Manhattan. It's a neighborhood of chic little boutiques, wood-paneled restaurants and singles bars. When I get off the elevator at her floor, she is standing in the hall outside her door to greet me. From a distance, in her blue-and-white checked dress, she looks of indeterminate age. Up close, I can see the white hair held back by a blue velvet bow, the pearl choker encircling her lined neck, the wrinkled face and arms. She looks up at me and smiles, her face alive with expectation.

She leads me to a peach-colored sofa, worn by time. "It's too soft for me," she says, sitting down on a straight-back, red-cushioned chair at my side.

As I set up notebook, pens and tape recorder, she goes to the kitchen. She returns with a tray holding two glasses of iced tea and a plate of chocolate-chip cookies.

Nature books fill the shelves lining one wall, representing a lifelong interest in conservation. Twelve file boxes, holding the membership records of the Friends of Central Park, are stacked next to the dining-room table. The table itself is covered with neat piles of paper— Estelle's office work in progress.

There are dried flowers in a vase, plants by the windows, two faded Persian rugs on the dark wood floor. Photographs of cats, of parks, of friends, are everywhere.

The air conditioner hums. As we talk the sun goes down and the room gets dark. The cookies are consumed. With a trembling hand, Estelle reaches for her tea.

She says that my questions are "tough," though she answers them after pause and reflection. "How interesting!" she frequently remarks as I share some of my own views about this project.

She apologizes because she can't remember the exact year when things took place. "Dates are elusive," she states, shaking her head and raising her eyebrows.

She tells me that her hearing is impaired by "nerve damage." Some sounds are difficult for her to grasp and understand. "This hearing business," she says, "is really quite frustrating."

M y main involvement is with the Friends of Central Park. This organization is interested in the preservation of historic parks. We have sixteen hundred members. We're concerned about maintenance, park upkeep and saving the trees. The city Parks Department doesn't have the personnel to do the work. We use some of our money for that. We've saved perhaps two hundred trees in Central Park as well as additional trees in other parks.

We save trees from dying by removing dead wood, pruning and fixing any holes that animals or time have made. We may spend six, seven hundred dollars on one tree. We hire private tree surgeons for consultation and then employ them to do the necessary work.

We get our money from contributions, from membership dues and from fund-raising events. Last week we held a moonlight bicycle trip. People assembled at two-thirty in the morning at the Guggenheim Museum, rode many miles and wound up having breakfast by New York Harbor.

A lot of people go to the park not to enjoy *it* but for a big event, like a rock concert. A lot of those activities could be held somewhere else. The big crowds do a lot of damage to the park. They litter. They tear up the ground. They don't care about preservation. We'd like to have people enjoy and appreciate their parks—to use them constructively, rather than destructively.

Every day I spend a good deal of time on membership. I get telephone calls from people asking for information. They've heard about us from a friend, or they've read about the organization in the newspaper. I'll supervise the mailings for different events, after coordinating date, place, leaders. I also do the filing for the organization. As we've grown, the paperwork has become enormous.

> *I cry sometimes when I get lonesome and*
> *think that I'm really quite alone—*
> *feeling that there isn't anybody whom*
> *I'm important to.*

I still like to go on some of the walks. Once or twice a wheelchair was provided for me. I didn't like it very much. Not only did I feel very conspicuous, but I also felt . . . incapacitated.

I have trouble walking now. I walk so slowly. I was mugged five or six years ago. When I was getting on the bus, a girl grabbed my pocketbook and me. I fell on the ground and fractured both hips. I'd been to the Museum of the City of New York and had crossed the street to get the bus home.

My purse has been picked a couple of times. I'm not so afraid on the street in the day. But alone at night it's something scary. When I get home I lock myself in. Then I think, if I were taken sick, no one could get in to help or take care of me!

I cry sometimes when I get lonesome and think that I'm quite alone—feeling that there isn't anybody whom I'm important to. There's also the apprehension that I won't be able to care for myself. I would hate to be dependent on someone.

I hear of so many good, attractive retirement homes. I have a friend who's in one. She has her own apartment in a building with other people her age. There's a dining room. She can have her car. They have programs. I think it's wonderful *for her*. She's there but she's completely independent. Of course, it's not cheap. But what is?

I can't bear to think of the rent on this apartment. It just went up forty dollars. Yet my superintendent told me that four or five people a day ask if there are any vacancies. Good apartments are very scarce. This is a very convenient neighborhood for me. I'd like to have a place where I could sit outdoors: a terrace, a garden. But the rent on something like that would be prohibitive.

When I go back to Grand Rapids, where I grew up, I long for New York. Grand Rapids seems so quiet. There are so few people I know; my close friends have died or moved. And the city has physically changed. The business is all out in huge shopping centers. On the main business street the stores are empty. The city has lost its core. Here, I'm right in the center of things.

My father was a pioneer lumberman in Michigan. Even though we had a very bad time during the Depression, somehow or other we seemed to have something left when it was over.

My mother was an active participant in causes. She was one of the founders of a guild that bought all the linen for one of the big hospitals. She was involved with one of the settlement houses. She lived to be 102. She was quite well the whole time. She had something to live for, a son who was ill, and I think she didn't want to leave him. I think that made a great difference. I'm convinced she prolonged her own life.

I had two aunts who were important to me as guides, who influenced the way I feel about things today. One was interested in nature. She used to teach me the names of the wildflowers and of the different birds. The other was very active in the suffrage movement.

> *My mother had something to live for, a son who was ill, and I think she didn't want to leave him. I'm convinced she prolonged her own life.*

My family was interested in everything. I was an active child. I always did things. I used to like to sew, to make my own clothes. I liked photography and was always taking pictures. I remember we played outdoors all the time. There were a lot of children living on our street. We did things together—skating, running games, physical things.

When I was quite young I liked to read. My mother, though, wanted me to be outside after school. So I'd just take my book and read on the porch.

My family was very sociable. We always had company in the house, my friends and their friends mixing together. Today it's quite different. Perhaps it's living in all these high-rise apartments where people really don't get a chance to *know* each other. People don't even *see* their neighbors. And the television has become the baby-sitter.

The only tip I could offer people who are lonely would be to keep busy. Be interested in *something.* And be with people. It's no excuse to say that you don't know anyone. You *join*—organizations, clubs. I still see some of the people I met on my first bird-walking tour in 1938. We had that in common, and then other things came along through the years. Whatever you're interested in, it seems to me, there's a group being formed or already in existence.

My closest friends have moved away and I miss them very much. But I know an awful lot of people because of my activities. I've met them through all the organizations I belong to. For example, I'm interested in politics. I'm a member of the Lenox Hill Democratic Club. I go to their meetings. I've served on a number of committees.

More and more I believe we shouldn't take life of any kind. I don't believe in the death penalty. To take a life is pretty risky business. You can't restore that. The alternative is to bring people up better, to give them better early training.

If people are dangerous to society, then I think they shouldn't be allowed to mingle with others. If they can't control themselves, if they're very angry and hostile, then they should be locked away.

I don't know whether I'm a liberated woman or not. I

know there are inequities, but I've never experienced them. I believe that if women want to have children, be interested in them, love them and enjoy seeing them grow up, they should stay home with them—at least until they start school. I don't think all women, just because they're women, are born to be good mothers.

Seeing women in all these political offices is strange. You have to get used to it. But I think they've been successful. To think that the mayor of Chicago is a woman! I hope she makes good. I don't know that women are any different from men in mental apparatus. I don't think I'll see a woman president, but it is a possibility.

I disapprove of women wearing pants. I don't see why they want to look like men. I don't even own a pair. In the cold weather, which I like, I wear woolen stockings and woolen panties. I just bundle up. I don't need to wear slacks!

I'm bothered about the clothes today. I think people look horrible. I like women to wear dresses with belts. I think that makes a woman look attractive. A belt gives her some shape. I can't get used to these slinky dresses with no petticoats. We always wore two or three layers of petticoats. We wanted our clothes to stick out, to look starched and stiff. But now they want them to cling, to be body-revealing.

I think men's pants are too tight. I read somewhere that the tightness is injurious—you know, around the genital area. And in hot weather men should take off their jackets. It's just silly to have them wear that extra clothing.

I lived in an era when sex was never talked about. I was very naïve. I'm not even sure where I learned about sex— possibly from friends. It even bothers me somewhat now to talk about it.

I don't think older people are sexless. I would enjoy some affection, some contact with people. But everybody's different. I'm sure there are some young people who lack an interest in sex.

I get up early, take the newspaper in from outside, read

it, and then go back to sleep. I'll get up again about nine, nine-thirty.

It's hard for me to describe an average day. I try not to do anything too regularly. I don't think some habits, some routines, are a good idea. For instance, if you can't eat lunch every day at one o'clock, you become very anxious. Psychologically, then, the dependence is no good.

I have no set bedtime. I think I'm a night person. I work better then. I'll go to sleep around midnight or later.

I like watching the news on television—anything that has to do with current events. I'm also interested in nature programs. A hurricane, now, that's something to watch! It's dramatic and terrible at the same time. The damage it can do is beyond imagination, yet it's also very exciting.

I eat anything I like. I try to eat nourishing meals. I don't eat junk food. I like to cook. I try to eat a variety of foods. A dinner might be a piece of meat or fish, fresh vegetables, salad and then fruit for dessert. It seems I've been eating a lot of ice cream lately. I think that's because it's so easy to keep and you've always got something on hand.

To feel good I take a private exercise class twice a week. A woman comes here, about an hour each session. I do stretches, some yoga-type movements. She does it right along with me. It also helps my arthritis.

Once a week I have psychotherapy, which I definitely think helps keep me in good health. I've gone for years. I lie down on a couch. The doctor's a man. I know that some people feel funny about this. They don't like to have it suggested. I think going to a psychiatrist or psychologist helps you understand yourself and other people.

I don't think anyone wants to die. But after you get so old, what other certainty in life is left?

I don't like to think about getting older. I take each day at a time. I've always been enthusiastic about what I was doing at the moment.

I don't think anyone wants to die. But after you get *so* old, what other certainty in life is left? I don't care about being buried. I don't care what happens afterward. I want people to be nice to me, thoughtful and kind, *now*. And I don't care what they say after I'm gone for that won't make any difference. I don't care about any memorials. There are lots of them around, in the parks. No one even bothers to look at them.

I'd like people to think that I was intelligent, tactful, agreeable and interested in other people. I think it's very boring to talk about yourself all the time. Some people don't listen very well. They just talk on and on about themselves. Well, I've got things to say too! But they never consider asking me what I do, what I think, how I feel about things. I guess the people who talk all the time are self-centered, and maybe they need you to be there for *them*. So sometimes, when I'm on the phone and I'd like to hang up, well, I don't.

I think I've had an interesting life. I was a social worker. I ran a tearoom. I was a photographer.

I think it was in the early thirties that I went to photography school. Then I worked for the WPA in Detroit. I was a professional photographer, a freelance, for a number of years. I don't think I was *that* important as a photographer. I took a lot of pictures of cats, because I liked them. And I took some theatrical pictures. That was by chance when I met some people who were interested in the theater. I took the cast pictures of *Golden Boy*. I guess that was my greatest theatrical achievement. Luther Adler, Frances Farmer, Lee J. Cobb, John Garfield, a lot of names—they all became very well known.

I sent some of my photographs to the archives at Simmons College. I was a member of the fourth class, when the school was first starting. They wrote back: "Had you sent us sixty-eight sheets of pure hammered gold we wouldn't have been so pleased. They are the oldest and most valuable pictures we have." I was terribly happy about that. Maybe my photography was more important than I thought.

When I got tired of my jobs, when they weren't interesting anymore, I quit. My family would support me. That made the difference. I guess I never really did earn my living. My parents subsidized me. Today I have income from securities. I think I'm very lucky, and don't you think I don't appreciate it.

I've never regretted not being married, not having children. I've built a life for myself, and most of the time I'm pleased with it.

Maggie Kuhn

GRAY PANTHER

In June 1970, Margaret Kuhn (known as Maggie) and five friends found themselves in similar circumstances. All were retiring from religious or social-work organizations. The group met to discuss their common plight, the future and their commitment to human liberation and social change.

The organization born that summer would draw its membership from younger and older adults. Initially, they called themselves the Consultation of Older and Younger Adults for Social Change. In 1972 the group became officially known as the Gray Panthers. The movement now has a nationwide membership of 35,000. One priority among their concerns for social justice is the problem of ageism—age discrimination and age stereotyping—and its relationship to racism, sexism and other oppressive, dehumanizing forces within our society.

Maggie Kuhn, the national convener of the Gray Panthers, is also a board member of many other organizations. They include the Senior Services Law Center, in

Boston; the National Council for Alternative Work Patterns; the National Action Forum for Older Women; and the National Institute for the Seriously Ill and Dying. She is a prolific author of journal and magazine articles, program materials and books, including *Maggie Kuhn on Aging.* And in 1975 she was the subject of a documentary film entitled *Maggie Kuhn: Wrinkled Radical.*

She was invited to visit the People's Republic of China in 1976. With other outstanding Americans, she was chosen in 1978 by the U.S.-China Peoples Friendship Association to serve as a tour leader. In the same year, for her unique combination of humanitarianism, social criticism and leadership, the *World Almanac* named her one of America's "most influential women."

Maggie is a tireless traveler with an extensive lecture schedule. In one recent month, she went to eight states and gave nineteen talks. Because of prior commitments, it took Maggie four months to get together with me. At first I was going to meet her on a train en route to one of her speaking engagements. Next, we were going to talk in the hotel where she would be staying during a Gray Panther conference. Finally, during a quiet week in early summer, I traveled to her three-story house in northwest Philadelphia.

Her home is on a tree-lined street in an interracial community, three blocks from the railroad station. There is a large front porch that seems to encourage visitors and good conversation. But the morning is cool. So I wait for Maggie on the mustard-colored sofa in the comfortable living room. There are two matching armchairs, a mustard-and-brown area rug, a coffee table heaped with books and magazines and an assortment of plants. A black-and-white cat stretches out on my knee as I sip my coffee.

Maggie shares her house with Linda, who is thirty-two; and with Bob, who is twenty-seven and married to

Bobbie, thirty-six. Each of the three floors is a self-contained apartment with its own bathroom and kitchen. These housemates pay Maggie rent, but they are more than tenants. They are friends. The relationship is the give-and-take among equals, with a sharing of comfort, caring and advice.

Maggie, at seventy-four, is frailer-looking than she appears on television. (I had first seen her on the Johnny Carson show.) Small and slim, she is dressed in a brown-and-blue plaid skirt, a lemon-yellow blouse and a navy-blue jacket. She wears her gray hair in a bun, tiny wisps escaping down her neck and cheeks. Her blue eyes are clear and alert behind half-glasses.

When I was born it was not uncommon to be born at home. In my case I was born in the front bedroom of my grandmother's home in Buffalo. For a time there were four generations living together, from my great-grandmother on down. This was certainly an example of the extended family.

I grew up in many places: Memphis, Louisville, Cleveland. My father was a hard-driving businessman. His company transferred him to many places. They'd move him at the drop of a hat. It was interesting to grow up in different parts of the country. My brother and I were as much at home in a Pullman car, in a lower or an upper berth, as we were anywhere. We got used to traveling. We all loved it. I still do.

I think my social consciousness developed from many sources. Perhaps a part grew out of an adolescent revolt against my father. He was a very authoritarian person. I couldn't accept a lot of his ideas, and I guess I just never got over protest as a form of revolt.

My mother was a beautiful, charming woman. My father adored her but he also oppressed her. She had to account for every penny he gave her. But he never gave her any *spending* money. My mother was a good manager. She graduated from college. She knew how to do things. I understood all this and it just made me so furious for her, with her. She couldn't break out of that pattern. But I could. She appreciated and understood what I did.

You don't retire from life. You just recycle and redirect your goals.

Working for the Y.W.C.A. was a very important influence in my life. This was in the thirties and forties. Two women who were my first bosses were ardent feminists. They were quite radical in their political thoughts. They were really socialists in their views. I was fascinated by them. The Y in those days was helping women organize in the labor movement. Women had not been encouraged to join. The labor movement was full of violence and hate and risk. There were a lot of strikes.

Eventually I worked on the national staff of the Y.W.C.A. From there I went to Boston to organize and work with Unitarian women. Then I went to the Presbyterians and stayed there for twenty-two years.

I worked in the United Presbyterian Church, in the office of church and race, and before that in the office of church and society. This was an exciting place to be and good preparation for an activist old age. The Presbyterian church tried to reach a consensus on issues. But in the fifties and sixties we built a social-action network, across the country, of people who weren't afraid to speak out, to take stands.

The Gray Panthers are bringing a special message to the people over sixty-five: "Look, you have the freedom to initiate change."

Officially, I could never make statements, give speeches or hold press conferences about the Vietnam War if they were outside the guidelines set down by the church's General Assembly. The General Assembly was as torn as American society was about the war. And some of us were saying, "We have to oppose it with everything we've got."

A number of us who knew each other quite well in New York were forced to retire at the same time. We had come together because of our involvement with the antiwar movement. We said, "In our old age we can devote full time and all the energy we have to fighting the Nixon administration and opposing the war."

All of us had been in fields of work with a social-action emphasis. It was natural that we would oppose the war. For a time it was not popular to criticize the administration. This was done at some peril. In the beginning it was a young people's cause.

We felt that, as older people, we had the freedom to do what needed to be done. This was one aspect of preparation for the new stage of retirement. You don't retire from life. You just recycle and redirect your goals.

We felt that in our old age nobody was going to stop us. Today I don't have to worry about what the General Assembly has said or not said. I can speak my mind. Before, the General Assembly usually ignored me. They can't any longer.

The name "Gray Panthers" was given to us by a producer at WPIX in New York. We liked it immediately. The initial response to it was, "It's a fun name. We'll enjoy it."

And then we discovered that it had a lot of public-relations appeal. It was allied in some people's thinking with the Black Panthers. We were tickled because that group was also making a very important protest, and in the early days we had some common goals. In Oakland, California, we even shared facilities.

The Black Panthers have never gotten a favorable press. The police beat them up and harassed them. This was particularly true in Philadelphia. They had an excellent hot-lunch program for needy children. But the police declared war on them. We said, "Wow, they're allies!" But then there was a sharp parting of the ways when the Black Panthers turned to violence.

The Gray Panthers are nonviolent. We are intergenerational. And we are not dealing exclusively with "old folks' issues." We're concerned about basic social change. We're not service-oriented. We are challenging why services are needed, and we're criticizing the way services are delivered. And we're bringing a special message to the people over sixty-five. We're saying, "Look, you have the freedom to initiate change. You're the ones in society who can do that."

I think my generation was programed to keep quiet, to accept things the way they were, to comply. We're trying to challenge that thinking.

When I taught a course on ethics and poverty at San Francisco Theological Seminary, I sent my students out to *find* the poor. How could they ever really learn if they only sat in the library and read case histories? This was a revolutionary move at the time because the students usually just stayed on campus and studied.

After the Vietnam War, there was a quiet time on college campuses. But I've been quite active speaking out across the country, and students are once again getting involved. They are concerned about the investment of university funds in South African enterprises. They believe, as the Gray Panthers do, that we cannot support racism.

The students are not raucous. They're not sitting in. They haven't gotten much press. But they're confronting their administrations and the trustees.

Young and old can and should work together for social change. Their needs and concerns are not mutually exclusive.

One of the most pressing problems I see at this time is better health care services for everybody. We need to radicalize the medical profession. I think we need to work toward some sort of socialized medicine. No one fusses about police and fire protection and schools. Those are public services we Americans feel entitled to. And health is a service we're also entitled to. The trouble is that we've made it into a highly profitable, lucrative business.

Another problem is inflation. We think there needs to be a critique of interest rates. We have challenged the Federal Reserve Board to change the regulations that put a cap on interest rates for small savers.

We'd also like to see people belong to food cooperatives, where you may save twenty to thirty percent. And you may get money back at the end of the year. Our house belongs to one called Weaver's Way. There are a thousand households in the cooperative. Five years ago it was a shoestring operation out of a church basement. Now you pay ten dollars a year for membership. You have to give certain hours of unpaid work: cutting cheese, bagging beans, stacking the shelves with staples. Not only do you save money and get a chance to have fresh produce, but it's a terribly civilized way to live.

Also I've been doing a lot of speaking recently on the energy issue. The Gray Panthers adopted a firm, strong position against nuclear power and weaponry at our convention in 1977. We've been marching. We've been raising our voices and our fists to say, "No!"

I think people are afraid to grow old because of the rigid age segregation that is so much a part of our society. One cause is mobility. Urbanization herds people together by class. Age raises the whole question of isolation by social class. Before, we never talked about it.

You see, the media have conditioned us to think that as we age we are no longer persons, lovers, attractive. We are certainly no longer employable. We might as well fade out of sight. But I think that is changing slowly as people become more aware of their options.

Don't forget, many people now in their sixties were young during the Depression. They were so affected by it, so convinced that they had to have money and things, that they vowed never to be poor again. That kind of conditioning makes you part of the system; these people are content, so they're not going to rock the boat. Linked with that is the sense of powerlessness; no matter what you do, you're not going to change it anyway. These are personal feelings. They go very deep for some people and we can't do anything about them.

Some women, though, are becoming radicalized in their old age. Perhaps they've been divorced, or they find out they don't have a pension. If they can get over the particular trauma, they can really turn things around. Unfortunately, these women in revolt are still a small minority.

My generation was programed to keep quiet, to accept things the way they were, to comply. We're trying to challenge that thinking.

I think older people should do with their lives whatever they wish. If they want to retire and do nothing, that's their own business.

The doctrine I've been preaching is one of interdependence and cooperation. That's a whole different value system from disengagement. The people who live in the fancy condominiums in Florida feel no identification with, or responsibility for, the people stealing dog food for their dinner. They're really disengaged, whether out of power-lessness or a feeling of preserving the status quo.

I've spoken to large groups of black men and women. And I've talked to them about the elders in China, in Mao's time. They were the ones who kept the revolution going. They remembered what it was like to be beaten by the landlords, to be sold for endless toil in the fields or on the docks. They remember the bitter past. And they talk about it. They keep it alive. Here, we relax. We've made it. We give up the fight.

Exposure in the media is very important. It gives me a chance to explain who the Gray Panthers are and what we're doing. I enjoyed going on the Johnny Carson show. I've learned to do it without being absolutely terrified. The first few times I was almost speechless. The media appearances have lost their terror as I've learned to do them. I think that's true of anything which at first is new or different.

Last year I did 117 one-minute television spots for a small producer who was starting his own company. I wrote them and they videotaped me. It took quite a lot of time. They've sold them to fifteen different stations. When I talked about health, I would suggest that you shop around for a physician, choose your doctor with care. I've talked about pets, gardens, plants, a lot of different things. At the end I would mention a book to read, a congressman to call or write, something for the viewer to do.

My generation of women still depends on men. I have no regrets that I've never married. I've been engaged three times. I've had lovers. But I've been very devoted to my career. If there was a man who really interested me, who could become a part of my life, we would live together. But marriage would take too much energy and time. I was the only one of my class in college who didn't immediately marry. They're all widowed now. They're all alone.

I think it's great if the marriage works. I like the idea of companionship. I think it could be delightful. But I feel good about not having that kind of closeness at the moment because for many years I took care of my mother, my father and my brother. And I worked hard at a demanding career at the same time.

We all lived together in their later years here in this house. I cared for them. They depended on me. I made a decision to have a loving responsibility toward them. There are a number of women in my age bracket who've never married who also made that same choice. In a sense they had no other choice. It was *assumed* they were going to take that responsibility.

The day after my brother was buried I fulfilled a speaking engagement, and I've been traveling ever since. This was in 1972.

Now I'm traveling with a new kind of freedom and purpose. I tell older people who are feeling lonely and depressed to stop thinking about themselves. Unless you reach out to an ever-widening community, circles that continue to expand, then in your old age, when the primary circle contracts, you may be the only survivor. If all through your life you've been wrapped up in your family, and then they die, and you've never developed any facility or any feeling of competence, you're stuck with yourself—stuck with your own memories, your own anger, your own angst. You think you have no future, only a lonely, miserable present. And you make everyone else around you miserable too.

I'd like to think that the reason I took care of my mother the way I did was because we were friends. I think our friendship meant that I understood my mother's relationship with my father. The tears come just to think of her. I know it was a tremendous sacrifice for her to let me go off on my own—to do what I had to do. She needed me and she loved me, but I was lucky that most of all she *knew* me.

*Young and old can and should work
together for social change. Their needs and
concerns are not mutually exclusive.*

For young and old alike I would suggest something
called a Life Review. The Life Review process gives people
a sense of their own history. By reviewing the past, a person gains courage, strength and hope to deal with the future.

You begin by drawing a life line. The area above the line
is for your private life, your personal existence; those close
to you are a part of that. Then below you write in the pow-
erful conditions, the influences of society. All of us are
shaped by both the private and the public factors.

The beginning of the process is to look at the year of
your birth. What was the situation in your family at that
time? In society? The closure date is when you feel you
may die. That's shocking for some people to even contem-
plate.

By looking back at the crises of your life, you see that
you've survived those. Why should you think you won't
survive what you're going through now? The Life Review
gives you strength and the feeling that you can cope. Look
at all the things you did, all the changes, all the disappointments that you've been through—and survived.

The Life Review shows what you've done, where you've
been, and lets you think about where you want to go. It's a
process of continuous change and growth.

I think I'll die in 1995. I think I can make it to ninety. I'd
like to die in an airport on my way to a meeting. I'm am-
bivalent about a funeral—whether I want one or not;
whether I'd like to donate parts of my body to science or
just be buried right here in my backyard with a party afterward. My favorite epitaph is one I read somewhere. A man

said, "Here lies my beloved wife, under the only stone she ever left unturned." That's darling! I'd settle for that if I had a tombstone.

I'm going to give this house and the one next door, which I also own, to the Gray Panthers. How about that? They can sell them—I hope they're worth something—or rent them out. Or they can use them as headquarters. So I'm taking care of things.

I also think we all should join memorial societies and work for low-cost funerals. People should take charge of their deaths just as they've taken care of their lives.

In my old age there's been a culmination and a gathering together of many strains of my life. Now I've put them all together into one solid thrust.

Margaret Mary J. Mangan

STATE SUPREME COURT JUDGE

Judge Margaret Mary J. Mangan is seventy-two. We arrange to meet at the State Supreme Court one morning at eleven. The case she is hearing is lasting longer than expected. Her law clerk shows me to a seat in the back of the courtroom.

Judge Mangan looks small behind the imposing desk, under the motto IN GOD WE TRUST. She wears a black robe over her long-sleeved green print dress. Her reddish-blonde hair, mixed with gray, is piled atop her head. Horn-rimmed glasses hang from a chain around her neck. She listens attentively to the testimony, with her right hand, pen laced through fingers, bracing her chin. She interrupts the witness with a curt comment: "Answer the question. Just a simple yes or no."

The case is adjourned until the afternoon.

Judge Mangan's chambers are really a three-room suite. There are a library, an office for her secretary and her law clerk, and her own spacious office with adjoining bathroom.

Her own room *feels* official. Facing the large desk are

two black leather armchairs. Behind it are four deep bookshelves filled with law texts. The black-and-brown, wall-to-wall carpet produces a somber effect. A black lounge chair is placed in a corner next to a telephone stand. Two walls are covered by honorary plaques. The desk is littered with papers, law books, legal documents and piles of mail. In the middle stands a bottle of mineral water.

When Judge Mangan ran for reelection to the Supreme Court in 1976, she received the endorsement of all political parties and was found "outstandingly qualified" by every bar association. Some of her honors include Achievement Award of the Interfaith Movement; Award for Outstanding Professional Woman of the Year; Grand Marshal, Memorial Day Parade, Knights of Columbus; and the Career Achievement Award from the New York League of Business and Professional Women.

Judge Mangan smiles and laughs easily. Her light-blue eyes are highlighted by blue shadow. As we walk through the corridors of the courthouse, she's warmly hailed by everyone in sight.

Mathematics did not come easy to me. I wasn't good in spelling. I enjoyed talking and I had a big mouth. So I figured the law would be a good profession. This was a field where you could engage in discussion and argument. At thirteen, I made up my mind to be a lawyer.

My grandfather was a lawyer, but he never worked at it.

I went to a Catholic high school. The nuns frowned on me. They thought I was a tomboy. They were horrified to think I'd go into a man's profession. All their graduates, the smart ones, would choose nursing or education.

The nuns sent for my mother. She was very progressive in her way. And she said, "Well, Peggy wants to go in for law." And that was that.

My parents were always terribly supportive of my plans. They were Irish immigrants. Life to them was a struggle. They really didn't know what being a lawyer meant.

My parents were wonderful, decent human beings. They came here from County Kerry, Ireland, when they were in their twenties. I was an only child.

My father worked at the Metropolitan Museum of Art. When the museum opened the Cloisters in Fort Tryon Park, he became the head custodian and had his own staff. He loved beauty. My father was a good, kind, gentle man. He was soft-spoken, quiet, calm. He would empty his pockets for anyone who was down on his luck.

My mother was the vocal one. She made with all the jokes. She never lost her sense of humor. She was the one who saved the pennies so I could go to school. She was a woman who never complained, but just kept right on punching. My mother was a "lady," in the good old-fashioned sense of that word, at all times.

At New York University I signed up for a seven-year program—college plus law. After one year, it was costing thirty-two dollars a point, and we didn't have the money for me to continue. Some of my friends were going over to Brooklyn Law School. They would be getting out in four years and could continue college at night. So I thought that was a good idea.

I went along with them. I went to City College every evening. And shades of Allah! When I sent in my marks to be evaluated, I found they didn't give B.A. degrees to women! This was back in 1932. The alternative was to take a degree in education. But that's not what I wanted. Would you believe I never got a college degree? Now, over forty years later, I'm having my marks evaluated. At this point it doesn't make much difference. But maybe the paper would be nice to have.

Right from the start I had to work harder because I was a woman.

I needed to serve a clerkship in a law firm. Being a woman at that particular time was a definite hindrance. The fact that I didn't come from Harvard or Yale or a prestigious school was also a drawback. Luckily my father had some contacts with a number of law firms. I went out on interviews. They said, "You're a woman. You're going to get married and leave. Why should we train you?" It seemed I made the rounds for months. All I got was more discouraged.

In one firm I asked outright, "Why are you turning me down?"

The gentleman answered quite matter-of-factly, "We only accept Harvard and Yale people."

"On what theory?" I asked.

"That the best go to the best," he replied.

Sometimes I'd feel so depressed by all the rejection that I'd go to Tiffany's and spend twenty-five dollars. The best go to the best, right?

Inequality, discrimination—it was all there. But no one talked about it in those days.

I finally found a job through answering an ad in the *Law Journal.* That shows you how far you can get on contacts! Sometimes they're useful, and sometimes you've just got to get wherever you're going by yourself.

I haven't got children. That's a great disappointment. I know people who live a second life through their grandchildren.

At that time Russia had a "five-year plan." I decided I'd have one too. I figured I'd be five years in the practice of law with somebody, and then I was going to open my own office. My goal would be to devote my life to public service. I stuck pretty much to schedule. I opened my own office on East Forty-second Street. I kept thinking to myself, "Who will ever know I'm up here on the seventeenth floor?" But somehow, through the little things I did for people, more people came to my office—a little case here, another one there. The word spread.

I realized that, to prepare myself for public life, I'd have to be politically connected. I went to the Democratic party as a real idealist. I was offered the nomination for registrar of New York County. It was a "woman's" job; that was an unwritten rule. I headed the whole Democratic ticket. And I won! I held the job for two terms.

I was still practicing law. I became Democratic state committeewoman, then chairman of the assembly district. I continued to serve on various Democratic committees, getting experience in all areas of political life.

Right from the start I had to work harder because I was a woman. When I was a practicing attorney and got up to argue, there was a stillness in the court. I'd say to myself, "Mangan, they're either waiting for you to make a fool of yourself or they're listening out of curiosity. Don't disappoint them either way."

If you do the best you can, and devote yourself to your work, I believe you'll get where you should be. Doors will open. You'll move to the next plateau. When I decided to get on the Supreme Court, no woman was on the staff except in the pool of stenographers. So I took the civil-service examination and passed. I became a court attendant. Frankly, they didn't know what to do with me. But I persevered and began the climb to become a judge.

In 1962 I was one of two women judges nominated to the Supreme Court. It was a novelty as far as men were concerned. I think we had to be *just* that much better. It's as if we carried a greater degree of responsibility. In regard to judicial decisions, the men would say, "For a woman, that's good."

I grew up in my professional life in an era when the males were dominant. When you got into that professional life, they ignored you. How could you not be frustrated? I suppose the time hadn't arrived.

Our Supreme Court is the busiest court in the world. We handle all kinds of actions—matrimonial, trusts, the dissolution of corporations, litigations often involving tremendous sums of money. There've been sessions that can only be recalled now as "blockbusters." I've handled up to sixty tough cases in two months. We have to keep that jam-packed calendar moving. Believe me, it's hard work.

The public thinks a judge's life is glamorous, the way it used to be portrayed on "Perry Mason." But we go till five o'clock, hold conferences on cases other than the one we're working on, conduct hearings—and then try to attack some of the mountains of paperwork. There are moments when I feel that I'll never get out from under it all. In my compulsion to get things done, I often work myself to fatigue. Yet I consider my stick-to-itiveness—never giving up, no matter how great the odds—to be a strength.

Now we have eleven women in the entire New York State Supreme Court. I guess you could say that progress has been made in the elective system itself. I don't feel I'm biased in favor of the women lawyers who appear before me. A professional shouldn't have any emotions. By and large, with a few exceptions, the women lawyers are conscientious and do a good job. I think these women are being recognized as responsible people.

Life has a way of retiring you—through your energies.

From my observation, the women's movement has been strident. It certainly hasn't been ladylike! But it has served a purpose. It has focused attention on the rights of women—the fact that brain power has no sexual identification, that a well-qualified woman should be as acceptable as a man. It's sad to see that some women do not realize they're not considered equal under the Constitution. How they could oppose a simple amendment saying that we're equal—that *now* we're only second, third, fourth-class citizens in the United States—is incredible to me.

I think that individuals can make a difference. And women should engage in politics on every level. That's what makes a democracy.

Now I'm going to say something very strange for this day and age. I do believe that a woman who is married should give her first concern to her family. If she can, without sacrificing, take an active part in politics, that's all well and good. It's an individual decision.

I never married. I guess I believed the saying, "Law's a jealous mistress." With my goals I knew the pitfalls that were ahead. I belonged to the school of thought that went: "If you try to do two things, one or the other will suffer." In my day and age I couldn't see having both a family and a career. I do recognize, though, that some women can combine the two.

At this age, in a way, I do regret not marrying. I never was one to be anxious about the future. And if you're in good health, you don't realize you're getting old—until someone says, "Oh, I'm so glad you made it," or "At your age, you're remarkable." You visit friends who were vital people, but now they're sleeping their lives away in nursing homes. It's scary! If my health breaks down, I have nobody. All my loved ones, my relatives and friends, have gone.

I haven't got children. That's a great disappointment. I know people who live a second life through their grandchildren. With children you know there's someone there who cares. There's a family unit. That's something I haven't got.

After the workday is over, I engage in a number of different activities. I go to professional dinners, fulfill speaking engagements, attend social functions. A really good evening for me would be to remain home and look at the "idiot box." Or read nonprofessional books, or listen to music of my choice, or attend a health club for the good of body beautiful.

In my job, when you reach seventy, you don't have to run for reelection. Now I'm on what they call "certification." Provided there's a need for a judge, provided you're in good health, you get certified every two years until you're seventy-six.

I don't know what I'll do when my certification ends—perhaps travel. That's something I've never had time for. I used to say, "When I retire, I'm going to make up for everything. I'll be a real Auntie Mame. I'll devote time to self-improvement. If need be, I'll get a face-lift. I'll go in for the works."

But somehow fear has entered into it. I'm not the free spirit I was who made those plans. Perhaps I'll carry them out, perhaps I won't. What will I do in retirement? How will I spend my time? Those are very realistic fears that I have to face.

I think that my passion for causes will keep me going well into my later years. I wouldn't think of self then; I'd think of the issue. The only problem is, how many causes are there?

Now I'm involved with the Equal Rights Amendment. Gloria Steinem is my ideal of women's lib. She speaks well. She's educated. She's poised. Not to denigrate Bella Abzug, but she's a little abrasive. She needs some polish. That abrasiveness rubs some people the wrong way. And if they're turned off to her personally, they're going to tune out to what she says. Her heart may be in the women's movement, but she antagonizes people.

*One of the benefits of getting older is
lived experience—and the accumulation
of 20/20 hindsight.*

It's trite, but basically the most important thing is your health. I still play tennis, I swim, I bicycle. Frankly, I don't miss out on anything, except perhaps that I've lost some of my bounce.

I'm five foot seven. I weigh between 120 and 150—but that's on a very bad day! I have three different sets of clothing to accommodate my changing size. I love to eat. And all the social functions I attend don't help me diet.

At my health club I'm into yoga. I can stand on my head. I tried calisthenics but found it to be too bruising. With yoga, it's just breathing, bending and stretching.

Time has passed, and I don't have the energy I used to. It's a shock to think, as I've gotten older, that I'm no exception. With the added years I just can't keep going at the same old familiar pace. Life has a way of retiring you— through your energy level.

When I think about it today, I guess I studied law primarily to do good. But it's not easy. When you're young, you have ideals and like to think of yourself as doing good in a big way. As the years pass, you learn that the only good you can do is in a small area around you. It seems to me that one of the benefits of getting older is lived experience—and the accumulation of 20/20 hindsight.

Because of my background and training, religion plays an important part in my life. I attend church regularly— out of love and out of fear. Isn't it great that we're not duplicates of anyone else? That we each have our own individual soul? You can't look at the sky and the trees and not know there's a God.

I feel life should not be prolonged by artificial means,

but that no one has the right to act as God in taking of life. But I have mixed feelings about capital punishment. I feel bad about swatting a fly. Yet a part of me believes we should have this law on the books—that it *is* a deterrent.

I've made no plans for my own death, except that I feel I should make a will. I know that Lord Mountbatten, and the late Winston Churchill, made plans for their own funerals. All I would want is a Mass said for the repose of my soul.

I'd like to be remembered as one who never was found wanting when the chips were down.

Lil Levine

FRIEND OF MUSIC

Lil Levine bustles around the small kitchen of her two-bedroom apartment (partly subsidized by her grown sons), preparing our lunch. The radio is tuned to a station that plays classical music twenty-four hours a day. Music has been and continues to be a major focus in her life.

The soup she has prepared, using her own secret recipe whose ingredients she won't divulge, is ready. We move into the dining room. The table is set with place mats of white lace. After the soup, we eat the salads she made earlier in the morning. The salads display a variety of colors and textures. "I like food to look attractive, to be appealing," says Lil. "I think it should be colorful and carefully displayed."

We sit and talk, facing each other in flowered armchairs at one end of the large, blue-gray living room. A gentle breeze comes in through the open windows. Eleven flights below, a cruise ship is visible moving up the Hudson River. There's a wood-burning fireplace. Oil paintings hang on the muted gray walls. One set of

built-in shelves contains books. Another holds stereo equipment and Lil's collection of records.

Lil is a petite, full-figured woman with short, gray-white hair. Her eyes are pale blue. She wears no make-up. She is dressed in a navy-blue shift, with a red necklace and matching earrings.

Lil's voice is strong and clear. She does not hesitate or mince her words.

My childhood was one of great poverty and hardship, of denial—denial of toys, of food. Inside of me, a voice said, "Tomorrow cannot be worse. It must be better." I arrived here from Russia when I was about nine years old. It was a terrible trip and we picked up vermin on route. I had to have all my hair cut off. When I started school the other children called me "boy-girl." It was an injury beyond human endurance, one I've never forgotten.

One day I was on my way home from school and I saw a fire-alarm box. I turned it. Before I knew what happened, I heard the engines coming from all over. I picked up my little legs and ran as fast as I could to my house. For a while it plagued me. I had the feeling the police would come and find me. It was a childish prank that was really kind of terrible. I never did it again.

I felt very unattractive and unwanted as a child. I had very few friends. I was squelched. At eighteen or twenty I never felt I belonged any place, never felt secure or loved. It seemed I went from place to place, taking care of sisters, staying with my brother. Looking back sixty years, I'd say my early life was sad, poignant really. It seemed I was always reaching out for something, but never getting it.

My older sister married a physician and then died giving birth to her third child. I moved in with my brother-in-law to raise the children, and then it didn't take very long for me to marry him. He was fourteen years my senior. I was twenty-four then. Having married him, I felt for once in my lifetime that someone cared for me.

From then on, little by little, I began to gain confidence. My husband was a man who loved his work, a remarkable man who was revered and respected. Soon, with his love, I began to come into my own. There were some stormy times with the children, especially the daughter who was only six years my junior. But that's all water under the bridge. I had no children of my own. I don't think I wanted any. Our family was complete and there was no need for them.

I think that divorce is due in large measure to women's lib. It's because men and women compete against each other.

My husband's dead now almost thirty years. He was one in a million. I could never have replaced him. There were chances, but I didn't take them. As a single woman, I don't let anybody dictate to me. I live my life as I would like, going places when I feel like it, meeting a great variety of people. If there was someone at home, I couldn't just get up and go. I couldn't get as involved as I do in other people's lives.

I'm eighty-two. I fill my life with people of all ages. I have many fascinating and gifted young friends who share their activities with me. They're almost always musicians and actors. From time to time I've had young people, creative people, stay here with me. They use the spare bedroom. One pianist I had staying with me was simply marvelous. He got whatever moral support he needed from me, and I was enriched a thousandfold by his music and by his friendship.

I don't pick my friends from one age group. I'm more

concerned about personalities, about whether there's some common meeting ground. What goes into creating rich, deep, lasting friendships? I suppose it helps to be yourself at all times. Don't be cocky. Don't act as if you have all the answers. Rather, exchange experiences and keep an open mind.

I abhor self-righteousness in anybody. Not to be able to admit you're wrong is, to my mind, a tremendous fault. People who are so cocksure of themselves, who are continually patting themselves on the back can be terribly obnoxious. I find such people loathsome. I cannot tolerate them.

Music is my love, the sustaining passion and force in my life. I studied piano and voice, but never did anything professional. I regret that I didn't try harder to be more active as a participant. Instead I became an ardent, active observer.

Music to me is a spiritual experience. It is enriching. It has a sobering and noble effect. It does something to my spirit, to my emotions.

Music fills my life whether it's the radio or stereo. Often, musical friends drop by and there'll be an impromptu concert in the living room. I'm supportive toward all of them, whatever phase they've reached in their careers. I clip and save their reviews, attend their concerts. I'm there for them. In return, I've been introduced to many great artists. I've even traveled with one of my very special friends when she performed abroad.

Women's liberation doesn't mean a thing when one is old, sick and lonely. The only cures for those maladies are interest and great love.

If you're a beginning listener and you have a stereo, just listen as *background* while you do things around the house. Then choose something you like and play it over and over again. Really begin to concentrate on the sound. You could start with a Mozart opera which is so beautiful and so easy to take.

I could cry when I hear great beauty in music, such as Bach's B Minor Mass or one of the Passions. I just sit and listen to the exaltation, the inner joy. I could sob, especially if I'm in a sensitive mood to begin with.

I am *there* for my family and friends . . . provided I love them. I think I would consider that aspect of my personality as a strength. Yet, at the same time, I don't think I'm a truly giving person. My givingness must be coupled with love. When I love there's no measure or length I wouldn't go to. I don't spare myself. There'll be times when I'll say, "Good God, I'm not the girl I was. If only I didn't have to do it." But I can't seem to separate myself from the people and things that give me such enjoyment.

Not being able to say "No" at times is almost torture. I can't recall the last time I said it. If I have a date that I really cherish or have made special plans, and then my granddaughter calls, I'll go to her. There is no choice.

And taking care of children today requires not only endless patience but a lot of physical stamina. I don't feel quite capable of coping with it to the degree that I used to. I love children dearly, but my patience is not as great as when I was younger. Last weekend I was with my great-grandson. He hurt himself. And I scolded him. He looked up at me and said, "You didn't even take the trouble to find out if it was my fault."

Well! At that point my guilt knew no bounds. I felt humiliated and ashamed. I'd like to be able to rectify that. I felt like a blooming idiot. He was hurt. It was my job to soothe him. Here's a baby who shows you your frailties.

My day is really quite loose. I have no set times to do anything. Perhaps I'll get up at nine-thirty. I'll clean the apartment, meet a friend for lunch. I'll go to the opera, listen to my records, read. I love biographies of great people. I want to know what goes into the making of a genius, what the struggles were, the joys, pressures, problems, passions.

I've learned that accomplishments come from a certain ability, drive and need. Things don't just happen. You have to want something badly enough to reach out for it. You may have to pave the way for yourself. You have to have great strength to break through. But when the goal is reached, when the drive is met, the success of accomplishment is unbearably sweet.

Sometimes I stay up until one at night. I love Dick Cavett's talk show on television. He's a very scholarly guy. He's interesting, scintillating, makes you think. He handles his subject so well. There's always something you can mull over and take away with you.

I've been blessed with a good constitution. Age has brought no dietary restrictions. I eat anything from herring to hot dogs. My refrigerator is always filled, and I'll whip something up for guests at the drop of a hat. My door is always open. I love having people visit.

I'm not ashamed of or afraid of anything. This is my life. Take it for what you will. Here I am. Sure, I'd like people to love me, but I don't care anymore about making an impression. Basically I'd like to always be what I am.

I think religion is extremely difficult to define. I think it's a spiritual feeling. It's trying to identify with something. Call your God whatever you will, it's something to hold on to. I don't practice religion. Yet I can't say I'm an agnostic. I do believe there's something beyond comprehension. But the answer is within yourself.

I believe I'm a peaceful person. But there are situations in which I would recommend capital punishment—for instance, for anybody who would kidnap a child of five or six and then molest that child and kill it. Anything short of murder, he can stay in prison.

I think there's an extraordinary restlessness in society today. There isn't any solidity. There isn't direction. People seem to be without hope. They seem trapped by not knowing how to conduct themselves to obtain some measure of peace of mind. It's as if they're running through a maze to some undefined goal.

I've told my children not to put me in a home. I'd like to stay here surrounded by the things that have given my life meaning and pleasure.

I think the women's movement as it is viewed by many is a sorry mess. I think the home and the family have suffered greatly because women have sought to strengthen their own egos. Keeping a home is a great undertaking, a great chore. I think many women underestimate that. It used to be that the home was the center. The children were all-important. You dedicated your life to them. It was a devotion filled with love.

And then the rebellion began. I can understand the frustration—the pull between career and children. But if you decide to have children, then it is necessary to care for them, nurture them and really be there, at least for the first ten to twelve years. That is not a job that's menial. There's great satisfaction to be derived from being a full-time mother. Children need their mother's love and security. They don't understand the pull of ego and self-aggrandizement. Children can feel abandoned. And a housekeeper is only a stranger at best.

I think that divorce is due in large measure to women's lib. It's because men and women compete against each other. It's because of great friction between two personalities fighting for power. This "lib" has been a tremendous obstacle in working out the family structure. Someone must be prepared to give, to compromise, and the woman must be the one to do it. If she wants to work, so be it. But don't be a mother too!

If two young people marry, they must realize it's a tremendous undertaking. Newlyweds to make a success of their marriage should exercise patience, selflessness, endless control and great tolerance. I don't think there's any substitute for a long-lasting relationship. The rewards cannot be measured.

I think parents should never live with their grown children. There are too many divergent interests involved. Try as you might, you still feel as though you're cramping their style. I can only see it as an added burden. It's no one's fault. The independence you've established throughout your life would just no longer be possible. That's a fact. It's wonderful to know that your children may want you to live with them. But for me, I pray to God that that day will never come.

And the old girls, the elderly ones, don't need women's liberation. Liberation doesn't mean a thing when one is old, sick and lonely. The only cures for those maladies are interest and great love. Those things keep people alive and well and vital.

"Sexy" to me can mean personality, color, something that's projected with nothing stilted or held back. It's got to be alive. It's got to have vibrance. People who have those qualities at ninety, I'd consider sexy. The age is irrelevant.

As for the term "senior citizen," I don't believe in labels, in something that categorizes a group, that sets them apart. The only thing about these people is that they're on in years. I don't think "senior citizen" is a very attractive label; it separates people rather than bringing them together. I think other people are frightened of them as a group, assuming that there'll be no common meeting ground. But that just isn't true. If you keep growing with the times, then there'll always be something to share.

I don't believe there should be a mandatory retirement age. For some people, it means a certain death. They must work to survive. It's a need for them. Life will become empty and dull and unproductive. You just sit and stagnate. I say, "As long as you can keep going, you should keep going."

I don't think people really change that much from when they were young. Perhaps you could say one emerges. I certainly did.

I cannot stand dullness, which is unfortunate. In fact, it's not very charitable. I cannot tolerate ordinariness. I need a life that's not stagnating, not just sitting and letting time pass. I don't choose to live or to die bit by bit. You should find something vital, something that enriches you, the thing that is closest to your heart. With me it's music.

Depression, fortunately, is a condition which need not last. One must try to lose oneself in reading, opening up to friends and looking for some avenues of escape. Grief, depending on what has caused it, varies. It depends on the severity and nature of what has created the grief in the first place. It is an endless battle, and one can only hope that time will offer relief.

I am aware of my old age, but I don't harp on it. Since I've enjoyed life so richly, I'm now more than ever aware of my mortality. I don't enjoy growing old. I anticipate ill health, a time when I'll be a victim to loneliness. I'm afraid of losing independence, needing help, being a burden.

If I were to die, I'd like to go fast. Enduring a death day by day would be a dread and a terror. And I've told my children not to put me in a home. That would really be unbearable. I'd like to stay here surrounded by the things that have given my life meaning and pleasure. When the time draws near, I'd like perhaps to have a companion, someone who shared my interests. That would make the end . . . not quite so bitter.

There's no recipe for how I feel. Perhaps you could call it a talent for living? I don't think people really change that much from when they were young. Perhaps you could say one emerges. I certainly did.

In my middle and later years I've been fairly gregarious and made friends easily. I'm enthusiastic about life. I have a quality of up and go. I'm so happy there's nothing troubling me that I'm busting out of my own skin.

I asked for little and I got a lot. I count my blessings. Of course there are situations in life that cause great anguish and great pain, but you surmount them and go on to the next thing.

I'm happy for the privilege of having been born, for the good and the bad of it. There's been a tremendous amount of color, a lot of drama, a lot of sadness. It has all added up to a rich life.

To sum up, I have learned a great deal, but there is ever so much more to challenge me. If I have not succeeded, it was in spite of trying. After all is said and done, we are, for the most part, ordinary mortals.

Pauli Murray

PRIEST, LAWYER, AUTHOR

The Reverend Dr. Pauli Murray lives in a garden apartment in Alexandria, Virginia. I arrive, somewhat breathless and out of sorts, feeling I've been taken the long way around by my Washington cab driver. Pauli draws a map for me as we try to figure out the route the cab took.

When Pauli Murray was sixty-six, she was ordained as the first black female Episcopal priest. She had already received two law degrees and an honorary doctorate from Dartmouth. She had served as deputy attorney general of California. She had published *Dark Testament,* a book of poetry; *Proud Shoes,* an account of her childhood in North Carolina; and numerous law-review articles. She had also been a founding member of the National Organization for Women (NOW).

She speaks of her sparsely furnished two-bedroom apartment as "a small library with a single bed." Custom-built bookcases encircle the living room. The books are organized by subject: poetry, black literature, Americana, Negro race, law books, civil liberties, civil rights, cultural mores. **The dining area is her office. Here are shelves and shelves of reference books and books on religion. The second "bedroom" contains a number of three-drawer file cabinets and more books. This room is primarily devoted to material about women. "Having a fancy apartment," she says, "isn't important to me. My money has gone into buying books."**

We sit on a white bench at the picnic-style table in the living room. A small television set rests on one shelf near the window. There's a comfortable-looking black leather armchair. A large black Labrador retriever lies quietly on the hooked rug, ignoring us for the major part of the day.

Pauli moves restlessly as we talk. She sits on her knees, straddles the bench, stands and leans her elbows on the table. Frequently she jumps up to find a photo album or book to demonstrate a point.

At sixty-nine, Pauli is five feet two and weighs 110 pounds, the same weight and trim figure she had at the age of twenty. She is a wiry, spirited woman with short, tousled gray hair. She wears glasses. She is dressed in turquoise jeans and a navy-blue, short-sleeve turtleneck sweater. A pale-blue enameled cross hangs around her neck.

Pauli's smile, a wonderful wide grin that reaches her eyes, expresses great warmth and interest.

When I was sixty-two, I decided to apply for holy orders. That was in 1973. Actually, retirement was only a few years away. It wasn't as if I were giving up a career. What I was really saying to myself was, "How do you want to spend the rest of your life?" And, in a way, it was a continuation of something I had been led to throughout the years.

I had been teaching law and politics at Brandeis. Students would make appointments to talk to me about their courses or their papers. Invariably, what they really wanted to talk about were their personal problems. When we talked about those, and worked toward some resolution, whatever bothered them about their papers just disappeared. On reflection, I realized I was providing personal ministry, personal counseling, even then.

I do a lot of counseling now over the telephone. It's very often just asking the proper questions and letting people talk the problem out. I get calls from around the country. This happens frequently enough so that I can say I have a telephone ministry.

Economically, I'm retired. I have my pension as a university professor combined with Social Security. The two together provide me with a very modest, no-frills existence. This allows me not to depend on the church for a living. Therefore I am what is called a "worker priest": someone who gets his or her living from elsewhere but is available for all kinds of volunteer work. Once a month I conduct the services at an old-age home. Or I might cover for another priest when that priest is out of town.

When I entered the ministry I made a commitment— that God would use me as he saw fit. So I don't really make plans, such as: "Next year I'll do this and then I'll do that." If that were my attitude, then I wouldn't be able to spend time with *you*. You and your letter are part of what's sent to me from day to day.

I see my life as a pilgrimage and a growth process. I don't see one achievement as being greater than another. As far as I'm concerned, they are steps along the process of growth. In terms of total personality, being ordained a priest was important because of what it represents in terms of my own commitment, my own spiritual development—and what it means in terms of women's sense of movement forward, into a fuller life.

I date the women's movement from the sixties, from two events: the President's Commission on the Status of Women and its report, which came out in 1963; and Betty Friedan's book, *The Feminine Mystique,* which also came out that year. I maintain that the president's commission acted as the catalyst. Its report was the first governmental document in our time that dealt specifically with women. It brought together, both in the commission and in the seven consultative committees (I served on the committee on civil and political rights), a collection of professional women and some men in many walks of life. It served as a very high level of consciousness raising. I remember saying to myself, "Meeting with these women, and seeing them perform, make me proud to be a woman."

I was too much my own person to want to be subordinate to anyone. It would have been impossible for me to be a traditionally married woman.

I have great admiration for any professional woman who is married and has children. The choice I made was not that. I was too much my own person to want to be subordinate to anyone. It would have been impossible for me to be a traditionally married woman. I have not had to make that choice so I don't stand in judgment over women who do make the choice to combine home and career. I simply stand in awe because I think it's tremendous to be able to satisfy all the responsibilities inherent in the two.

I applaud the newer generation of women who are trying to find ways of working this out, of sharing responsibilities with a husband. The whole concept that *each* should have time off, that the husband should be involved in the nurturing and caring of children, is marvelous. The burden is not entirely on the woman, as it had been. I think it depends on the individuals, on their training, their economic status, the wife's expectations, the husband's expectations.

I grew up in an intergenerational family. My grandparents were the heads of the household. There were six of us. Our parents died when we were all very young. I was three when my mother died. I was separated from my brothers and sisters and went to live with an aunt in North Carolina. Another aunt took the two babies. The three older children stayed with my father in Baltimore till he became ill and died.

As I grew older, because I was separated from my brothers and sisters, I longed to have a family that was *my* family. I went around either "adopting" other people or having other people "adopt" me. I developed friendships with the mothers of my girlfriends. One mother called me her "second daughter." So I got a sense of sisterhood, of being a part of someone else's family.

My grandfather died when I was almost nine, my grandmother when I was thirteen. Both my grandparents died at home. They were nursed up until their last days.

I had more than thirty second cousins and assorted third cousins. We lived in the same small town. So I had a sense of extended family. You gave the older people great respect and reverence. And you were responsible to all of your adult cousins. Any one of them who saw you doing something wrong reprimanded you, and then reported you to your elders. So I was always aware of supervision and authority—so much so that today I give deference to my older sister. There's only two years' difference, but she's now the oldest member of the family.

I have eight nieces and nephews. I've had the joys of motherhood and none of the responsibilities. On balance, I'm not sure it's necessary to have children physical in order to enjoy young people or have a sense of interaction and a sense of passing on tradition.

The issue of respect is different today. Urbanization has tended to disintegrate the extended family. People move away from their roots in search of employment. The aging process segregates people who outlive their physical mobility and who get put away in nursing homes. All of these factors tend to cut away at the family structure.

From about 1920 to the mid-sixties a whole generation

of women grew up under the idea of being in the home, of having children, of being mothers. There was less emphasis on career. These are now the older women who haven't had a chance to catch up with the changes that are taking place. These women are the "displaced homemakers."

Of course, the movement has been strident. What movement *isn't* strident? Some Negroes used to say, "We have the right to be mediocre, if that's what we wish." In my generation, you were constantly trying to prove that you were equal as a woman—and you turned out having to be *superior* as a woman. You had to be three times better than the male. Now women are beginning to say, "We want to be human. We want to be able to make mistakes or not be the best and to be accepted as a human being at whatever level we are in life." I would think that much of the stridency that comes out of women, very much as with blacks, is when you suddenly realize how much you've been deprived.

In a sense, this too is progress. People have reached the point where they no longer accept inequality. As they begin to make advances, the anger comes—with the realization that it never should have been that way in the first place.

Mrs. Roosevelt said, "Don't push too fast." And I said, "You're not going fast enough for me." Out of this stormy interaction grew friendship.

I didn't go out to challenge Harvard Law School. I didn't intend to sue them. It just worked out that way. I won a fellowship for graduate study in law. The tradition was that the top person, the one who won the fellowship—and they'd all been male—was to go to Harvard. I was sim-

ply following the tradition. I was so naïve I didn't know
that Harvard didn't admit women. So I applied. I get back
a letter saying, "Dear Miss Murray: Your picture and the
salutation on your college transcript indicate you're not of
the sex entitled to be admitted to Harvard Law School."

Well, there I was, a young graduating law student—and
there's nothing more arrogant than *that.* I appealed. It was
wartime and the faculty was decimated. They decided to
make *no* decision until the faculty returned. Meanwhile, I
went to the University of California for my law degree. Six
years later, in 1950, Harvard Law School began admitting
women students.

No, I don't think I make stands. I wasn't challenging just
for the sake of challenging. What's important is the particular situation. Suddenly, in the attempt to carry out what I
considered the normal activities of life, I would find myself
hitting these barriers.

In 1940 I was traveling with a college friend in Virginia
on a small bus. The custom was that Negroes filled up the
back and whites filled up the front. My friend and I were
sitting on a broken seat, so we moved up. The driver told
us to move back. We told him about the seat but he never
came back to check. He stopped the bus and went for a policeman, who wrote out a summons. The policeman told
the driver to hold the summons in case we gave any more
trouble.

The driver distributed witness cards to all the white pas-
sengers: "Did you see an accident? Who was at fault?
Would you be willing to testify? Your name and address."
I said, "Driver, why don't you distribute these cards back
here? Are you discriminating against us?" At that point he
went for the police again. This time they arrested us.

We were charged with disorderly conduct, creating a
disturbance and violating the segregation laws. They
threw us in jail for three days. We had a hearing and were
fined. The NAACP stepped in. We were going to challenge the segregation laws and take it to the Supreme

Court. At that point the state withdrew the more serious charges. But we were convicted of disorderly conduct. We refused to pay the fine. So we stayed in jail until the organization I was working for decided I was more important out than in.

There was that kind of tradition in my family—to be proud. They didn't tell me to stand up and fight for my rights. Their whole attitude was, "*We are somebody.*" After taking and taking and taking injustice, there comes a time when *this is it.* Once you say, "No more," then you tend to act.

I trained to be a civil-rights lawyer. So it was natural, when I then ran into sex discrimination, that I would also challenge that.

I like the word "Negro." It stays capitalized. I'm from the generation that fought to get it capitalized. It's a nice shocker for people today who never hear it anymore. But I also say "black."

In a total and absolute way you couldn't say that in our century there's been more discrimination against sex than against color. Women have not been lynched, per se, as women; women have not been physically brutalized and killed. Women have not been actually enslaved, in terms of bondage. But later a black woman would suddenly find she was not really benefiting by many of the opportunities accorded her race—because of her *sex*. It's called "double jeopardy." I seem to have encountered more difficulties because of my sex than because of my race.

I think it's the saddest thing in the world that the Catholic church does not recognize women priests. Episcopal women are supporting Catholic women in their struggle. I look at the Pope with mixed feelings. He seems so loving, and yet he has this traditional attitude. It's a real theological blind spot.

I might, personally, have great problems with abortion. It would be a moral and ethical and spiritual problem for me. However, this does not lead me to say, "A woman should not have the right to make that decision." I think she has the right to wrestle with that problem with herself, her maker and her doctor.

I wish we could find alternatives to abortion. When I was doing my clinical pastoral education as a seminarian, I worked as an assistant chaplain at Bellevue Hospital in New York. Two of the wards I covered were gynecology wards. I saw some of those young women recovering from abortions. I thought there ought to be another way—some preventive action. Why not concentrate on the male?

I am against capital punishment. I was once associated with a case where a man was sentenced to the electric chair. For two years we sought to get the sentence commuted. I visited him in the death house, in Virginia. His cell was the last one before a short corridor leading to the door to the area that housed the electric chair. I kept thinking about the proximity of the electric chair and the barren surroundings—and that this poor man sat day after day contemplating the fact that one day he'd have to walk through that door.

If I had not seen that, I might have a theoretical view. But maybe my religious convictions also play a part. Have we the right to take what we cannot give? I am committed to nonviolence, in the Martin Luther King tradition. I'm not prepared to take a life that I cannot replace. I can't ask another man to throw a switch that I can't throw.

Have I ever been lonely? Loneliness is a part of living. We'll never lose it. Younger people have it. People feel it in the midst of crowds. A certain amount of loneliness is inherent in the human condition.

The real contribution that older women can make to younger women is to give them the sense of continuity.

I've been lonely a great deal of my life. But I've learned to live with myself and learned to have things to do. There's enough stuff on my desk to keep me busy for I don't know how many years. When I feel sorry for myself, if I pick up the phone and call someone and ask how they are, by the time that person gets through telling me their troubles I'm feeling better. Giving, reaching out, are ways of not being desolate, of not being lonely. When I preach at the nursing home I tell them, "You have a ministry right here: just a kind word to the next person."

Women fear aging more than men because of our cultural conditioning. They have not been accepted as single, unattached women. Yet this is what the older generation *is* because of the great discrepancy in life expectancy. We really have an aging population of women.

Aging can be the recognition of our mortality. I am now the older generation. This becomes even clearer when all around me friends, colleagues and relatives of my age group are dying. I went to the fiftieth reunion of my high-school class. There were forty students to begin with. Eleven made the reunion. We counted seventeen survivors. These are my contemporaries.

I'm beginning, just this year, to have my first serious arthritic threat. This left foot is bothersome. Among the things we have to face as we grow older are the gradual physical restrictions. I'm aware of that, and I try to plot my life accordingly.

For example, I don't accept every invitation given me. I try to space my week so I have no more than two commitments. I will turn something down if it means two days in succession. I simply know that I don't have the energy. Mainly I don't want to become a problem to myself and other people. And you *can,* if you live alone. I try to keep myself going because there's nobody else to take the dog out. The dog becomes a measure of discipline. I have to take him out three times a day. He's my responsibility.

I'm usually awake at five. Don't forget I come out of a

farming background. When I was in school, and even as a teacher, I'd get up at two-thirty, three-thirty. But I'd go to bed early, get a good night's sleep, then get up and do my major studying and preparation in those quiet hours of the morning.

I'll have fruit juice, toast and coffee around six. I'll take the dog out at six-thirty, trying to avoid the traffic and other dogs. Then I like to dawdle, to read the newspaper. At around eight, I'm ready to begin my day. I tend to carry out the same discipline as if I were working in an office. It's usually writing, preparing a sermon, doing the research for a speech. Around twelve, twelve-thirty, out *he* goes again. I come in and have lunch, just a simple sandwich, peanut butter, brown bread, maybe some soup, a bottle of beer. Then it's back to work. Around six, six-thirty, I take the dog out for his last go. Then I tend not to do any more work, unless it's some emergency. Occasionally I will watch television. I try to hit the news each evening. And throughout the day I'll spend a lot of time on the telephone.

I'm a lousy cook. I simply cook to live, to keep myself going. I have had some intestinal problems and am supposed to keep to a bland diet. I don't go in for fancy foods. I'm a meat-and-potatoes person. My dinner is the one good big meal of the day: maybe baked chicken or chopped steak, a green vegetable, a salad, some cookies, a bottle of beer. I don't eat junk food and I don't eat between meals.

I have thought about my death and made preparations. I have directions attached to my will, specifying cremation, the Episcopal service, the hymns. When I did all this I was in New York. Now someone will have a problem getting me there! I have a plot where two aunts and a dear friend are buried. All they have to do is take up a little plug and put in an urn. My name is already there, on a plaque. I got that idea from Eleanor Roosevelt. After Franklin Roosevelt died, they put up a simple large tombstone, giving his name with his date of birth and death, as well as her name with her date of birth. When she died, all they had to do was put in the final date.

When I talk about Mrs. Roosevelt I'm probably talking about someone who was not in your immediate experience. I talk about her in the sense of reality, not as a person of history. I knew her for about twenty-two years. Mrs. Roosevelt was the guru of my generation. I don't know any woman today who equals her stature.

Mrs. Roosevelt encouraged and admired my generation of young activists. For her, I think, I represented militant Negro youth. And since she was deeply concerned about civil rights, she liked me. As we both grew older, we grew closer. But of course the racial picture was changing too. She said, "Don't push too fast." And I said, "You're not going fast enough for me." Out of this stormy interaction grew friendship.

Younger people can bring a certain amount of vitality, a special kind of adventure. Through them, older people can project into the future. There are great areas of life in which I'm thoroughly ignorant—for example, computer science. *You* are growing up in a world I never grew up in. There is much you can tell me about the kind of world in which you're functioning. And it's changing so fast. I'm just fascinated by young people and the kinds of skills they have.

Older people both give and get when they associate with young people. They would be ill-advised to assume that because "I have lived or because I am older, you should listen to me." Age does not necessarily bring wisdom.

Hopefully, my life will have touched somebody else's. The real contribution that older women can make to younger women is to give them the sense of continuity.

GRACE CHU, *left, cooking teacher and author:* I don't hide my age. I don't sit here and moan, "Oh dear, now I'm eighty." I rather enjoy it. The Chinese people have respect for older people. So if you were to go to China and say you were eighty, you could probably do many things you couldn't do here.

HELENE PAPANEK, *below left, psychiatrist:* I don't have a secret power to make people feel better. They come here because they have flaws. They learn to accept their flaws. I like them as people in spite of their flaws.

HELEN BORCHARD, *below right, sportswoman, college student:* People are afraid of getting older because they fear they won't be able to do the things they used to. But I don't think that senility has to accompany old age.

FLORENCE GOLDMANN, above, director of a senior center: At this stage of my life I don't feel threatened. I don't think I'm ever going to stop achieving, because that's me. But I'm no longer looking for recognition.

FRAN LEE, above, consumer activist: I get up every day and know I'm going to get bruised. The majority of people have a "Don't rock the boat" philosophy. Well, I can't accept that. I see life as a crooked picture and I want to straighten it.

PAULI MURRAY, right, priest, lawyer, author: Have I ever been lonely? Loneliness is a part of living. We'll never lose it. People feel it in the midst of crowds. A certain amount of loneliness is inherent in the human condition.

MARGARET MARY J. MANGAN, state supreme court judge: After the workday is over, I engage in a number of different activities. I go to professional dinners, fulfill speaking engagements, attend social functions. A really good evening for me would be to remain home and look at the "idiot box," or read a nonprofessional book, or listen to music, or attend a health club for the good of body beautiful.

Yetta Cohn

RETIRED RADICAL

Yetta Cohn has worked as a social worker, as a police-woman and as a business executive for mail-order firms. During one period she owned a restaurant on Fire Island. Her philosophy for success was: "If you came in for a Coke, you got the same treatment as if you bought a bottle of champagne."

Yetta lives in a spotlessly tidy, one-and-a-half-room apartment on the East Side of Manhattan in, she says, "shabby gentility." There's a minimum of furniture—antiques, carefully preserved.

Four years ago, at the age of sixty-five, she was diagnosed as having emphysema, an illness that changed her lifestyle. "I can't walk a block without getting out of breath," she says as we sit down to breakfast on a rainy morning in October.

Yetta is a tall, handsome-looking woman with ear-length silver hair. She wears a yellow pants suit and white flat shoes. We sit at the large, round dining-room table, the scene of her Monday-night poker games. She urges me to add some lox to the cream cheese and bagel already on my plate.

She talks quickly and becomes angry at herself when I probe for a date. "When you get to my age, you forget—goddamn it!" I express concern about her cough. But she just shrugs, pauses for a sip of coffee, lights up another cigarette and continues where she left off.

She is a spirited, passionate woman, a believer in causes. "I'm a retired radical," she says with pride.

The most exciting part of my life was in the thirties. I have grandnephews. They're square. They have no battles. The most exciting thing for them to do is go to a wedding in Rochester! They're against pollution. Well, that's like being in favor of mother and apple pie.

In the thirties we were fighting for the Spanish Civil War, for home relief, for Social Security. We were fighting for causes that had meaning. I was one of the first organizers of the State-County Municipal Workers. I took part in the first sit-in at the Department of Welfare, the first sit-in in New York City. We worked in Harlem. What could be more exciting than that? It was a ball.

Being a Jew you learn how to fight. It's part of your heritage. It's inborn. In the thirties I was against Zionism. But Hitler made me a Jew. Now I'm for Israel.

I was a social worker at the Department of Welfare. The salary was some ridiculous figure like thirty dollars a week. Along came the police exam, and the salary would be higher. Fifteen thousand women took the exam and three hundred passed. There were separate exams at that time for men and women. I became a policewoman in 1940. We were sent to the Police Academy for training. They didn't teach us anything—except, if you're driving a car and you hit somebody else, give them a ticket first! Charge them with disorderly conduct! It was ridiculous.

The second week I was in class, a lieutenant came in and wanted to know who wore size fourteen. I raised my hand. He called me outside and asked if I played poker. I said, "Yes."

So he assigned me to the World's Fair. I replaced a policewoman who was being transferred. With a male partner I did a jujitsu act. I was absolutely terrified of getting on that stage before three thousand people twice a day. This was an official exhibition by the New York City Police Department.

The Police Department was politically inspired at the time. You had to know someone to get a decent assignment. The Juvenile Aid Bureau, where I wanted to be, was considered a "plum assignment." I never got into it.

The women's movement is the best thing to happen since the wheel.

I decided I had to get myself noticed by the director of women. She was a very bright woman with no education to speak of, but a real war-horse. I wrote a column for the police magazine, hoping to get her attention. I even mentioned her name. I was given the job as her assistant. I was a go-fer—go for coffee, that kind of thing. I wrote her speeches, pretended they were hers and became active in the policewomen's association.

The 1940 class brought in a lot of college-educated Jewish women. Up until that time the department was mainly Irish, Catholic and terribly bigoted. When they revised the magazine I got a job working on it. That was delightful. I came and went as I pleased.

I left the Police Department in 1952. I quit because of all the harassment. My phone was being tapped. It's a complicated story, but in essence it involved my friendship with someone who was called before the House Un-American Activities Committee. The Police Department called me in for an investigation. They wanted to know if I was a member of the Communist party. Where did I live on certain dates? I was frightened. Remember that this was an era of terror. They never charged me with anything, but I was so terrified that I resigned. It was scare tactics. How do you prove you're not, when they say you are?

After the Police Department I went to Europe for a while. I wasn't quite sure what I wanted to do. My experience had always been in civil service. When I came back I took a job with a mail-order house. I'm a good organizer. I worked terribly long hours and Saturdays and Sundays. I finally couldn't put up with it and left to start a mail-order division for another firm.

I don't believe in working seven days a week. At first, when I take over, when things are in a mess, I do it—let's say for two months. But after that—no weekends, no overtime.

This new outfit was handling junk mail. Someone has to put those little packages together. They told me to hire fifty people and get all the machinery. I didn't know what I was doing, but I didn't tell them. I had the guts to try it. Why not? I'm a quick learner. I figured that in three weeks I'd know what to do—and I did! After two months things were going beautifully.

But I learned something. If you're running a business, just because everything is going smoothly, it doesn't mean you relax. You have to examine it again and ask yourself, "How can I improve it?"

I used to dress very carefully. Generally, as the sole female executive, I found it very important to be the best-dressed woman in the office. I spent a lot of money on clothes for work. When I retired I decided I'd never get dressed again. I'm just going to slop around in whatever I feel like. Today I don't care about clothes, as long as I'm neat and clean.

The women's movement is the best thing to happen since the wheel. It's done so much for young women it's incredible. I'm just sorry it didn't happen when I was in my twenties. You had to work so hard as a woman to be recognized, to get any place. I see these young kids earning fabulous salaries, working at marvelous jobs.

The only liberals around now are those who haven't been mugged.

I don't think the homosexual issue has anything to do with the women's movement. It's an entirely separate item. I hate the word "gay." I prefer the word "homosexual."

I think that homosexual women did better in careers than heterosexual women—that being a homosexual, unsaid, unspoken, was an advantage. Your employer knew you didn't have any children at home, knew you could stay overtime, knew you had to make it because you didn't have a husband to help support you.

I don't go someplace and announce I'm a homosexual. What's the point? I'm a human being. I act properly. I dress properly. I'm not violent. I'm a nice person. You accept me as a human being. I've always gotten loans at banks, up to forty thousand dollars. I bought a co-op. I bought property. I've run businesses. I never had to announce I was a homosexual.

After a while people understood it. Nobody ever dropped me as a friend—even my own family. When I was invited to dinner it was understood that I'd bring whomever I was living with. They may not have wanted to talk about it, but it was accepted. And I've never chosen my friends on the basis of their sexual preference. What they do in their bedroom is no one's business but their own.

My father died when I was nine. My mother was a fabulous woman. She supported four daughters. We had a dry-goods store. I was behind the counter from the time I was seven. My mother was up at five and never went to bed before midnight. She was politically illiterate. All she cared about was seeing that her daughters got an education. That was terribly important to her. She wanted us all to be schoolteachers because that was the highest profession a woman could hold.

She died when she was eighty-seven. She was very independent. She never took a nickel from any of us. She was so concerned with making a living that there was no warmth, no time for us. I recognized it. My other sisters didn't. They hated her, and they ruined their own lives by becoming very cold people. Within her own limitations my mother was a great woman.

I left home when I was nineteen. My sisters were all married. When I was in my thirties my mother said to me, "I don't understand how you live. But if it makes you happy it's okay with me. I don't want you to be lonely."

Once, when I went home to dinner, she gave me a check for two thousand dollars. I had money. I didn't need it.

I said, "What's this for?"

My mother said, "When your sisters were married and I made them weddings, I spent two thousand dollars on each one. I know you're not going to get married, so I want you to have the money."

My mother had a sense of fairness, and an acceptance of my lifestyle. She adored the woman I lived with for twelve years. When we broke up, I didn't know how to tell my mother.

I feel money is very important. You have to put a value on yourself. The money is a symbol of how you think about yourself.

Sometimes I regret not having children, from an ego standpoint. It would be carrying on an image of me. But at the same time I felt I would be a terrible mother. I'd probably demand perfection. I'd probably want my kids to be the best at everything.

I've just gotten to know some of my grandnephews. That's after twenty years of noncommunication because of the difficult relationship with my sisters. The kids are okay, solid middle-class citizens. They think I'm the black sheep who knows interesting stories. They think I'm the greatest. One grandnephew cleans this apartment every Saturday.

I was active and healthy most of my life. I was an athlete. As a kid I got paid for playing basketball. I was the captain of all the teams. When I was nineteen I thought "Who wants to be a female jock?" So I turned into an intellectual. The worst things that ever happened to my health were a strep throat and a broken arm.

But four years ago I got emphysema. I never counted on being sick. I was rushed to the hospital. I was sure I was dying.

I thought to myself, "Here I am; I can't breathe. I'm not afraid to die. I think I've lived a good life. I've done more than the average woman. It's been fun—a lot of ups and downs. I've met marvelous people." Then I became angry. I wouldn't be able to collect on my Social Security! I wouldn't be able to go over to the senior-citizens home with the 144 used decks of cards sitting in my closet.

When I got home from the hospital I started to feel sorry about some of the things I *hadn't* done, such as learning to sail a boat.

The emphysema has changed my life. If I had good health I'd be fabulously happy. And nobody really cares how you're feeling. You're going to tell someone who calls up that you're feeling lousy? I learned that no one listens. I used to have breakfast at a coffee shop where they knew me. The cashier was always very pleasant. She'd say, "Good morning, Miss Cohn, how are you? That's nice."

Well, one morning I said, "I think I'm dying."

She said, "That's nice," and continued making change.

I think that our society has changed so much in the last twenty years that we're living in a jungle. I'm for capital punishment. If these people had scarlet fever, you would isolate them until they were cured. We don't do that. We put them in jail, and they're out in three years, and they're not cured!

What does it cost? Forty thousand dollars a year to keep someone in prison? I'd rather see the money spent to keep our libraries open for two hours more a week. Give the money to programs for gifted children to expand their horizons. The only liberals around now are those who haven't been mugged.

I feel money is very important. You have to put a value on yourself. The money is a symbol of how you think about yourself. Once I learned that a man I was working with was making three thousand dollars more than I was. That put me in a huff. I went to our boss and asked why. He answered, "Because he's married and has two children."

I said, "I've got a mink coat and my old age to take care of."

He increased my salary.

I was a product of the Depression, which put a scare into you about money. When I earned fifteen dollars a week, I saved one dollar a week. But sometimes I made extravagant gestures. One year I gambled on the stock market and made sixty thousand dollars in three months. But in five months I lost eighty thousand dollars.

I read voraciously, even cereal boxes. I never go anyplace without a book.

The goal was to live out your life comfortably. The idea that I wouldn't be able to afford a decent apartment, food, clothes and medical bills scared me to death. I think every older person's fear is that the money will run out. I think it's criminal that little old ladies are starving. It's the government's fault. They should make an allowance that would keep every old person in the country living above the poverty level.

What I hate most about old age is the indignity of it all. If you're not well and you don't have money, old age becomes a humiliation. I'm terrified of being a bore—of repeating myself, of being testy, of hating young people, of always looking to the past. I don't want to grow old like that.

I'm resentful of getting old. I can't adjust to it. I fight it. My advice? You've got to keep at it. The only alternative is death.

I think you have to learn how to ask for help. And if you never ask, you'll find life tremendously difficult.

There are certain basic fears about getting older. I'm afraid, because I live alone, that if I die in my sleep I won't be found for days. I want to be able to take care of myself; I don't want to be dribbling down my shirt. I want to be able to cook my own meals. I don't use instant coffee. When I do that, I'll know my life is over.

I get up at six-thirty. I have an internal alarm clock. I have the papers delivered; that's one of my luxuries. I make coffee and read. I read voraciously, even cereal boxes. I never go anyplace without a book. Then I call my broker and check out my stocks. The day goes very quickly. I used to think television was the idiot tube. But now that I'm in the house so much I find I really enjoy it. I try to be a selective viewer. I love the tennis matches, documentaries, anything educational.

I love poker. I have a regular game here every Monday night. People arrive in the midst of the worst blizzards. These are very bright people. Poker is a fascination: a combination of skill and psychology. If you know how to play your cards you can win with garbage. If I was healthier I'd play every night in the week. It's tremendously exciting.

I've become a letter writer in my old age. I read the papers and write to people when something upsets me. I wrote a letter of criticism to Ambassador Andrew Young at the United Nations. But I'll also write with praise when something good happens.

People have to learn to take care of themselves. I was in analysis for two years. If I had a bellyache I'd go to an internist. If I had a toothache, I'd go to a dentist. So when I had an emotional problem, I sought out an analyst. I definitely think people can benefit from this kind of help. It taught me a lot about myself.

I've made a will. It was after the death of a friend who didn't have one; the small estate she had went to an uncle she hadn't seen in thirty years. I want to be cremated and have my ashes scattered over Fire Island. A friend once said, "You'll know how good a person you are by the number of people who cry at your funeral." Yet I will have no funeral. If your funeral is on a working day, people have to take time off from work. And I don't want to put anyone out. And if it's on a weekend, it eventually turns into a very boring cocktail party. I'd like to think people will be sorry I'm dead, and that they will look at me as having been a good person. I've written my own obituary thanking the people *I* wanted to thank. It begins with the boy who sent me chocolates for Valentine's Day when we were in the fourth grade!

I think you can be deeply influenced by certain people you know. And I was lucky to know some great people. There was Moses Soyer, a painter from the famous Ashcan School of art. And for many years I was the friend and confidante of Judy Holliday, the well-known actress. I knew dancers and writers. I even played poker with Gene Kelly, Oscar Levant and Maureen Stapleton. If I hadn't known them, I don't know what the hell I would have been. Maybe a housewife in the Bronx?

I think people should indulge themselves. Take that trip to Europe. Don't wait. Spend the money you have on yourself. With emphysema I shouldn't be smoking, but I do. I eat Chinese food, ice cream and cake—anything I want. You've got to have fun.

I've always believed in two things. The first is hard work; you've got to have discipline in your life. And, second, I believe in having a good time; I want to be tired from having fun.

Florence Goldmann

DIRECTOR OF SENIOR CENTER

Florence Goldmann is the director of the Northwest Multi-Service Senior Center in Margate, Florida. At sixty-seven, Flo is responsible for preparing and implementing budgets, supervising and evaluating a staff of twenty people and assessing the needs of older persons in Broward County.

The center is open to men and women over sixty, Monday through Friday, from 9:00 A.M. to 5:00 P.M. The sprawling one-story building houses a range of activities including ceramics, yoga, dancing, painting and woodworking. There are classes in physical fitness, weight control, transactional analysis, world affairs and human sexuality. The 4,300 members are offered hot meals, vision and blood-pressure screening, a telephone reassurance service and legal counsel. The programs are funded under the Older Americans Act through the area's Agency on Aging and Florida's Community Care for the Elderly Act.

The poster on the door to Mrs. Goldmann's office

reads: "Love everyone unconditionally including yourself."

Flo, five feet, two inches, her short, thick brunette
hair streaked with gray, smooths the skirt of her
brown-flowered cotton dress as she stands behind her
desk to welcome me.

Her eyes dance as we talk, her face alive with spirit
and enthusiasm. She conveys an impression of strength,
speaking without pause, her tone self-confident, her
hand pounding the desk for emphasis.

The phone rings several times. Staff members peek in
to ask questions. To all she is reassuring and patient. I
feel I'm in the presence of a take-charge person: the director of my summer camp, the house mother at my college dormitory.

In the auditorium where center members are having
lunch, a volunteer plays the piano. "Shine On Harvest
Moon," "Easter Parade" and "Yankee Doodle Dandy"
provide musical background to our talk.

When we lived in Great Neck, Long Island, I
was on the school board, served as director
of the United Community Fund, was on the
board of the Great Neck Senior Citizens Cen-
ter and also did their public relations. I've always been a
very active person.

I became interested in older people while I was president of the North Shore women's division of the American
Jewish Congress. The congress in New York brought out a
directory of services for the Jewish aged in the city. I
looked at the directory and said to myself, "We've got to
have something like this for Nassau County." At that time,
Adelaide Attard was the director of Nassau County's Department of Aging. I made an appointment to speak with
her. I showed her the book and told her I felt we needed a
directory of services for *all* aged, not just for the Jewish
aged, and that I didn't have the funds to print it.

She said, "It's really exciting you should come in right now, because I have plans for something just like that, and I don't have a PR person to work it through."

We made a deal. I told her I'd do the book, on a volunteer basis, if she would give me a staff person to bring me up to date on the county's resources—and if she would have the book printed. She was ecstatic. So for three months I worked on it, writing and typing it at home and then brought it in to her.

She surprised me by asking if I'd ever thought of working in the field of aging and taking a paid job. This was in 1972. "Flo," she said, "I think you're wasting your talent."

This would be my fourth career. I had originally been a teacher. I taught commercial subjects in high school for fifteen years. I'd been training secretaries, so I didn't think I'd have a hard time getting a job.

We weren't sure whether Florida would be right for us. I loved my home, I loved my work. What can I say? My heart sank.

A month after I quit teaching I went to work as the private secretary to the president of a textile company on Seventh Avenue. And, you know something, it wasn't easy. Somehow the connotation of teaching wasn't very compatible with business in those days. It was 1945. My husband had just come out of the service, and I asked for a raise—for fifty dollars a week. Believe me, that was a big deal.

The job gave me a lot of latitude. I formed a sales-promotion and publicity department. The president died, and I was given more and more responsibility. I grew.

In 1950 suddenly, out of the blue, I found I was pregnant. I was forty years old. We made an arrangement for me to work three days a week. And then when my son was five I quit altogether, stayed home and became active in local affairs in Great Neck.

Then the aging booklet came along. And there I was as program-development supervisor for Nassau County's Department of Aging. When the Older Americans Act amendments were implemented, suddenly a whole new world for the elderly opened up. With Addie, I wrote proposals for federal funding.

The first grant was for $47,000. We had to spend it in three months or they'd take the money back. My idea was for an information and referral program in a mobile van that would go all over the county. I think we had about 150,000 people over sixty in the area at that time. I bought a secondhand twenty-seven-foot van for nineteen thousand dollars—the largest thing I could buy that wouldn't require a chauffeur's license to drive.

The dealer was so nice, and so enthusiastic about the project, that he said he'd rip out the whole interior and build it to my specifications. I wanted the kitchen taken out. Instead, I'd have a counter with chairs where people could fill out forms with someone to help them. I planned to staff the van with a social worker, a clerk and a field worker who would be the driver. I had a private consultation area with a door for confidentiality. We got the whole thing done, built and staffed.

It was a natural success. We scheduled it like a political candidate. On such and such a day, it would be in Westbury at such and such a location, at a certain time. The papers would publicize it and the Senior Mobile would be mobbed.

Then one day a man came to my office from the Long Island Taxicab Association. He wanted to do something constructive for the elderly. I enlisted his aid to help transport the elderly to the mobile van and back to their homes.

In those days, part of my success was the ability to think ahead. And part of it was timing and luck. There's so much fate attached to things. Everything was sailing along.

I got a new title, a raise. My son was in college. Everything was beautiful. And then my husband got sick and had to retire. He needed a milder climate. I gave notice. We weren't sure whether Florida would be right for us. I loved my home, I loved my work. What can I say? My heart sank.

Women, especially, fear growing older. If you look in the mirror and you suddenly see an old lady there, well, you're not very happy. But you can always put on make-up and look much better.

In the beginning, Florida to me was another world. I wrote letters trying to get a job—and nobody wanted me. Nobody. They either felt I was a threat, or I was too high-priced or they didn't know. I tried in the worst way to get even a part-time job. Down here they're political but they don't admit it. They're really a closed shop.

We went up north. Gus had an operation. We returned to Florida. We could live much more reasonably here.

I took care of him, during his convalescence, for almost eight months. Then I thought, "I've got to look ahead. I've got to get a job." Finally I was told there was an opening as an administrative assistant in the Agency on Aging. I interviewed for the job. I didn't get it.

At this stage of my life, I was going through the whole interviewing process all over again. I was very upset. I thought to myself, "My God, what I've forgotten, most of them don't even know yet." Four weeks later I was called about the job here. And this time I got it! This center was brand new. They'd just moved from a storefront.

I was sixty years old when I began to work with the elderly. I felt I could relate well to them. I was thinking in the terms they thought in. I was aware of the problems they were facing, psychologically as well as chronologically.

I didn't want this job just for financial reasons. We knew when we moved down here that we'd have to reduce our standard of living. I wanted something to do. I *needed* something to do. It's been a fantastic opportunity.

At the moment I'm working on the budget for our day-care unit. It's for senior citizens who are here during the day and home at night. Our program is keeping these people out of institutions.

Ours is a youth-oriented society, and not even the tremendous life experiences of older persons are recognized and appreciated. I think the media are at fault. You always see gorgeous pictures of these young, great-looking, beautiful, lovely little things flitting across your television screen. Now come on! How many people actually look like that? Maybe the reality of age isn't so great, but we've all got to face it.

Women, especially, fear growing older. You lose your looks a little bit. If you're vain and you look in the mirror and you suddenly see an old lady there, well, you're not very happy. But it doesn't have to be. You can always put on make-up and look much better.

Sometimes people have very bad psychological traumas with age. It could be the loss of a spouse or a dear friend. Or there could be a certain amount of family conflict: "Oh, well, that's grandma. She doesn't know what she's talking about."

In old age, some people cease to produce and cease to be needed. It's a time when work stops for a lot of people, so you don't have the driving force that you've got to be in a certain place at a certain time. Some people love that. Other people find themselves absolutely miserable. Along with the loss of work, there's a decline in income, so that economic problems become a major concern.

The whole Social Security structure is a little unfair. The

years people are really productive they can earn only up to $4,500. That's really insane in an inflationary period. I guess Social Security was not meant to be the sole income. If it's just supplementary to other income, that's fine. You can manage all right. But if not you're in trouble.

I think that older people who have given a lot in their lifetime, regardless of what it is, should receive something back when they're in need. It's terribly sad that older people in America are not treated with the dignity to which they are entitled. There has to be a change in the way we *treat* older people and in the way we *think* about them.

If health permits, old age should be viewed as a pleasurable time of life. Like most stereotypes, the idea that older people are sexless is definitely a myth. In many cases, the sex drive in older persons diminishes somewhat with increasing age, but it does not vanish. It can certainly play an important role among older couples and older individuals.

I enjoy reading about sexuality and don't mind sex in movies providing it's done in good taste. I'm not opposed to premarital sex or having couples live together—for people who are young adults, not for children or teenagers. I do believe that excessive premarital sex diminishes the "family concept," and I'm not sure whether this result is so desirable.

There has to be a change in the way we treat older people and in the way we think about them.

I think the years of my life which were the most stimulating, productive and pleasurable were my forties and fifties. I would not, however, like to go back in time. I must admit, though, that I'd like to think I could go on with my present life—in my present physical condition—for a long time to come. I've always felt that you get out of life pretty much what you put into it.

All women, in order to be really fulfilled, have to be prepared to make some kind of work contribution. It doesn't have to be for pay. There's a big gap that takes place in your life when you stop being needed as a parent. Even your domestic life shifts with your mate. You have to figure out what you're going to do in the future that's productive and satisfying. You must do more than just plan. You must equip yourself to do what the planning calls for. Sometimes it means going back to school. Sometimes it's just a brush-up course to get back the skills you had when you were younger.

Good retirement is very hard to come by. The person's own nature plays a very important role. I just happen to be the type of person who can't sit around. Pool-sitting and golf—I love them. But I have priorities. Those activities are fine for the weekend but I've got other things to do. My friends think I'm crazy to be working. But this is what makes me happy.

I have little opportunity for solitude between my rather demanding work and my desire to share free time with my husband of forty-three years. I like to read fiction, when I'm not writing or reading literature related to my job. I enjoy listening to music on radio and TV. I use solitary moments for personal and household chores. I enjoy cooking. Some of my spare time is devoted to writing a newsletter for my condominium association. And I have just been appointed to the city of Boca Raton's Community Relations Advisory Council.

I've been fortunate in my choice of mate. He'll tell you that I'm happiest when my mind is active, when I'm working and getting things done. And he wants me to be happy. He's healthy now. He's playing golf. We play nine holes together every Sunday afternoon. He has his own friends. He misses me sometimes when I'm at work, but he enjoys knowing I'm busy and active.

A great many people from the Northeast have moved here. It's unbelievable how we've all gravitated toward this area in Florida. There are about six couples we're friendly with. We see each other on the average of once a week.

The idea of marriage being fifty-fifty is for the birds. What happens if you're giving fifty percent and at that point the other person is only putting out twenty percent? Then you've got only seventy percent in all! Marriage is a constant give-and-take. I feel that way about life. You've got to be flexible. You've got to roll with the punches and be able to bounce back.

Generally I am very loquacious. But I become extremely quiet when I am depressed or grieved. I don't cry often—in fact, I very seldom cry. When I do, it's usually because of sad events, such as the death or extreme illness of someone dear to me. Or I may cry from complete frustration, such as my inability to cope with the actions or attitudes of my twenty-eight-year-old son. For instance, it bothers me that I haven't seen him in a year. I miss him. He graduated from medical school, married the next day and moved to Milwaukee. Hopefully they'll be visiting us soon.

Marriage is a constant give-and-take.
I feel that way about life. You've got
to be flexible.

At this stage of my life I don't feel threatened. I am no longer ambitious—*because* of my age. I don't think I'm ever going to stop achieving, because that's me. But I'm no longer looking for recognition or achievement in my field as a professional.

I've never made any issue of my age at any time in my life. Some women take off five, ten years when talking about their age. I guess I've been fortunate that people have always taken me for eight to ten years younger than I was.

I'm in great good health—knock on wood! I'm not yet compelled to think of myself as an "older person." I still take the problem of the moment and deal with it.

I am tenacious and I follow through on all my commitments. If I believe in something strongly, I'm going to fight for it. I have a facility for involvement. I feel I am a warm, outgoing, energetic woman, honest, forthright and considerate. I like people and I care about their problems and what I can do to help them solve those problems. I consider myself more of a "giver" than a "taker."

The old can offer the young experience, knowledge, a certain kind of wisdom from having lived through their lives and, I think, compassion. The young can offer the old hope, ambition, spirit and a certain amount of excitement.

Feeling that young people can do everything by themselves is ridiculous. They can't. They need guidance and help and support and love. If they don't get those things, they're never going to make it. Unfortunately, there seems to be a certain resentment among younger groups toward older groups and vice versa. But they don't have to be mutually exclusive. The needs of youth are just as important as the needs of the elderly.

When I stop having a job—when I feel I'm not as productive as I should be, or I'm getting too tired—then I would like to devote my energies to advocacy for the elderly.

I don't like to think about dying, so my plans are rather general and vague. We have a family plot in New York. I've told my husband I'd like to have some light music at my funeral, such as "I'll Never Walk Alone." I do not wish to have a traditional religious ceremony, but rather have a few very close relatives or friends speak for a few minutes.

I would like to be remembered by my husband as a loving and interesting wife. I would like to be remembered by others as someone who cared about people generally, and about older people in particular—and who tried to earn them the dignity and the better life which they deserve.

Helen Borchard

SPORTSWOMAN, COLLEGE STUDENT

Helen Marshall Borchard lives in New York City, in an apartment house across the street from Central Park. We meet on a day when she will not be driving out to her country club in Westchester. She is a prizewinning sportswoman who plays golf and tennis regularly. She appears fit and trim at five feet, two inches. Her face, arms and legs are richly tanned.

We talk in the air-conditioned den of her spacious apartment. It's a quiet room furnished in muted earth colors. A maid serves frosty glasses of iced tea with floating sprigs of mint.

For many years Helen performed as Wendy Marshall, the "Toy Lady," creating a profession based on her love of music and of children. Building on those interests, she founded the successful "Children's Entertainment Series" at New York's 92nd Street YM-YWHA. She serves as a board member of many organizations, including Family Day Care, Inc.

And last year Helen Borchard, seventy-six years old,

devoted grandmother of two, began a new career as a college student.

Fordham University's College at Sixty offers an opportunity to develop interests for the "retirement years." According to its brochure, the College at Sixty is open to "men and women over fifty who are free in the daytime and have (1) a capacity to learn from reading and (2) an inner urge to keep their minds from vegetating."

Each student takes one seminar per semester, choosing from the fields of philosophy, art, literature, science, economics and psychology. Upon completion of four seminars, the student receives a certificate. This allows the holder to enter Fordham's liberal-arts college without meeting additional admission requirements.

Most of the students share an enthusiasm for learning—for its own sake. They are studying not because they have to, but because they want to.

*S*yracuse, in upstate New York, was where I was born and raised. I have a sister who's a very brilliant person, a pianist. She played with Toscanini. She's now at the Juilliard School teaching English diction to singers. She's been there about forty-five years.

My father died when I was eight. My mother was a very forward-looking, intelligent person who encouraged us to do whatever we were interested in. I wanted to get married and have children. That was my main ambition.

Yet I became a children's entertainer. I had taken singing lessons while I was growing up. I knew that I would never be a Metropolitan Opera star. But I always thought children's songs were interesting. I thought maybe I could perform for the children confined to hospitals.

My mother had called me Wendy because I reminded her of Wendy in *Peter Pan.* That's why I became known as Wendy Marshall, the Toy Lady. As Wendy, I sang songs to children, using toys and props to illustrate the songs. I had a basic costume of white duck pants, a shirt and a necktie. And women in those days did not wear slacks! Then I'd add a hat or a scarf, things like that, and really *be* the character I was singing about. I did all the changing right in front of the children, and they loved it. I had a bunny costume. I had a merry-go-round costume with flags and horses; I turned around while I sang that song.

It was a participation program. I'd ask the children questions. They'd tell me what different touches to add to my costume. If I was going to be a cowboy, they'd tell me what to put on. We sang some songs together; some I sang to them. It was fun. I liked it.

After he died, I really realized I was an older woman. Together we had had a "young" life, doing the things we wanted, when we wanted.

I went to see a man connected with the Steinway piano people. I hoped he would recommend me as an entertainer to parents who were planning parties for children. He asked me to audition. So I did.

A couple of months later he called and said, "Mrs. Roosevelt would like to have you at the White House. Would you like to come?"

This was a Christmas party. A few days before the event, he called again. "Mrs. Roosevelt," he said, "wants to be sure this won't interfere with your plans for the holidays." That concern, that caring—they seemed so typical of her.

This was in 1933. President Roosevelt came to the party. He wanted to know whether I had had some ice cream and cake. Wasn't that considerate? I was thrilled. I changed my clothes in the Dolly Madison Room. Two years later I went back and gave another program. This time I changed my clothes in the Lincoln Room.

The children who came to the parties were friends of the president's grandchildren, Sistie and Buzzie. They also invited the children of the diplomatic corps. We decorated the whole East Room with balloons. Can you imagine? It was a first! A few weeks after each performance, I received a present from the Roosevelts. I still have the pewter matchbox with the presidential seal. It's in the other room, on the coffee table.

I performed for television in the early thirties, when it was still in the experimental stage. People didn't have sets at home. You could watch it in the studio or up two flights or down two flights, but there was nothing broadcast over the air. Every time I went on, they'd try a different color lipstick, or different make-up, to see which came over the best. I also had my own radio program. There were even fan clubs. This period in my life was great fun.

I went to a party one night, and a close friend suggested that a friend of his, Bernie, take me home. At two other parties the same thing happened. I was bored to death with Bernie. And he didn't seem to care either. But one day he telephoned me.

About two years later we were married. We had one son. He's happily married to a darling girl whom I dearly love. They have two children, six and four. They live in Westchester County, north of New York City. They come into the city or I go there. My son's been wonderful to me. He's a lawyer, a partner in a large firm. I come along with problems and he straightens them right out.

I've always wanted to be independent if I could, for as long as possible—not to be a burden on my son.

I can remember when he was a little boy. There were lots of older widows in my family and Bernie's family. They kept coming to see us. I used to say to Bernie, "Every night that we can close our door and be by ourselves, I relish."

We never had to provide a home for an older member of the family. But we would have been willing to, if necessary. I think it's awfully good for families to be a unit. Of course, personalities make a difference. Some people are much more interfering than others.

Last month I went on a tour to China. There, they take it for granted that the older people are part of the family. We didn't get to see any nursing homes. Our guide claimed there weren't any in China. But someone on our tour had a friend who had visited one. I'd hate to be put in a nursing home. But if it had to be, I guess I'd have to accept it.

I've had three cancer operations. If my life was going to be short, it was going to be a merry one. If it was long, I wasn't going to worry about things that never happen.

I'm pleased that I can be helpful to my children when they need me. I rang them up the other day and volunteered to be the sitter this weekend. Yet I try not to thrust myself on them.

My husband was one of the most energetic people I've ever known, a smart cookie and full of fun. We had a beautiful thirty-nine years together. There wasn't a morning when I didn't wake up with a laugh. He was in a business he enjoyed. He "retired" four times but went back to work each time. The last time he said to me, "I'm ready for it now." At that point he was seventy-eight years old. But he was *young*. Nobody thought of him as being that age.

Two months later, in May, he had a severe heart attack. I don't think it had anything to do with his retirement. He was in intensive care for two weeks and in the hospital for over two months. When he came home he was fragile, but he got over it.

In the winter he was feeling much, much better. He loved the Keys in Florida. He adored fishing. I wasn't crazy about it, but I liked being with him. So we went. We had a wonderful day doing nothing together. That night he suddenly just keeled over. It was unbelievable.

This was three and a half years ago. I haven't gotten over it yet; I don't think I ever will. Lots of women think their husbands are great. I *know* mine was.

I think I've *had* to become more independent because I'm more alone. When Bernie was alive I wanted to do what *he* wanted me to do. Now it's a case of making a life of my own—alone. After he died, I really realized I was an older woman. Together we had had a "young" life, doing the things we wanted, when we wanted.

I still see our coupled friends. And, yes, I do feel like a fifth wheel. It just kills me to go places and see couples, particularly older ones. I think to myself, "Bernie's gone, and *they're* still hanging around." That's a nasty thing to say and a nasty way to feel.

I have a lot of good friends who've been awfully sweet to me, very considerate. I try not to have them feel that I'm sticking around all the time. If we go out, play golf and have dinner somewhere, I don't want them to feel they have to pay my way.

I haven't met anyone I'd want to date—or who wanted to date me, for that matter. I don't see anything wrong in dating. Sometimes I miss a man in my life. But just go out with anybody? I never did that in my life. Why should I start now?

My husband said to me when we were first married, "Don't ever go to sleep being mad. Always kiss good-night."

Being single doesn't stop me from doing things. I just don't think I enjoy them as much. I still haven't gotten over the feeling of coming home and wanting to tell Bernie things. Going places together—I haven't gotten over that.

But in one sense I'm used to going places alone because Bernie traveled a lot. While he was out of town, I'd go to plays that I thought he wouldn't want to see. The other day I wanted to go to Lincoln Center. I called up a few people but no one wanted to go. So I went by myself. It was better than not going at all.

In the newspaper I read an ad about Fordham's College at Sixty. I felt that the oral-history program might be interesting. I didn't know the first thing about a tape recorder, which sounded very modern to me; I'm the most unmechanical person in the world.

The college got a grant for the program. And we got paid for our work! I never expected that. Oral history, the tape-recording of people's lives, is useful historically.

The College at Sixty has been great fun. I've gotten a lot out of the courses. I've made many new friends. It's like belonging to a club, only better. I feel very lucky to have fallen into it.

Last semester I took a course on preretirement and retirement. We learned that people have to prepare for retirement ahead of time. You have to prepare financially. If you want to move to another community, you've got to think about what you're going to do there, and with whom. You have to plan what you want to do with the rest of your life.

You shouldn't sit around by yourself—unless that gives you pleasure. After working hard all your life, you deserve to do what you want.

Meeting people isn't a problem, unless you never leave home. Go places; go to a Y; go to a school and take courses. Just get out of your house and *do*.

When I play golf I usually leave the house at nine. In the summertime we play Tuesdays and Thursdays. We play on those days because on the weekends the girls go away with their husbands. We'll play nine holes, have lunch at the club, then play nine more. I also play tennis there, and go swimming.

I've always been athletic. I grew up playing tennis and golf. I used to love ice-skating. My mother encouraged us to be active in sports. I've kept these activities up through the years.

I usually stay home in the evenings unless I've been invited out, or there's something I especially want to do. I don't cook for myself. I have a maid, fortunately. If I have to cook, I can. But I don't like to. I watch television. I read. I have a hundred things to do. I feel I never get caught up. I go to sleep late—twelve, one o'clock.

I've had three cancer operations. As a result I decided not to stop doing anything I wanted to do. If my life was going to be short, it was going to be a merry one. If it was long, I wasn't going to worry about the things that never happen. I never dreamt that I'd outlive my husband.

Perhaps his death has made me think more about my own. I've made a will. I'll probably be buried next to my husband. I don't give a damn about my funeral. My son should run that. I guess I'd like people to say, "She was a fun person who gave some pleasure to others."

I have mixed feelings about mercy killing. If it were for me—if I were hopelessly sick and a burden, a running expense—then I would want it. Whether I could go through with it for someone I cared about, I really don't know. In a way, I think there's always hope.

I've been very lucky that I've had a lot of energy. I can travel and not feel tired. Last month, after China, I went to Japan for a week and stayed in a convent. A woman I had met at Fordham is a nun. After being in the order for fifty years, she had her golden jubilee, with twelve priests and a choir. There was a party, and ten of us took her out.

She lives here now but taught English in Japan for about thirty years. She and I just happened to be visiting there at the same time. She got permission for me to stay at the "community"—that's what they call the convent. I lived in a tiny house with screen doors and windows, mats on the floor, a tatami to sleep on. You changed your shoes when you came in.

As for the Equal Rights Amendment—well, I think women have the right to equitable salaries. I think they work very hard bringing up their children and engaging in a career at the same time. The fathers who are good fathers spend a great deal more time with their children than they used to. That's a kind of role reversal.

When my son was growing up I was always able to talk to him. I could be outspoken and explain things. I'd say, "You don't do this because . . ."—and then give the reason. I think one of the troubles with families is that they *don't* give reasons. Teen-agers especially need to *know* how and why you've made a specific decision.

For instance, Billy went to Europe with two friends the summer before his senior year in college. A few nights before they left one of the boys came over to see us; he felt we were his second family. He said, "Why can't we go to Germany? My father says because . . . and I don't think that's an answer."

And I said, "I agree with you. I don't think that's an answer either." So I explained our reasoning: "We don't say you can never go to Germany. If you want to go with your own money when you're older, that's all right. But we're not going to pay five cents to the German people, because we lived through the war and it was devastating. We saw what they did and we're very much against them even though some of our antecedents were German. I had three German grandparents."

So you see, if people sat down and discussed things, tried to talk their problems out, I really think they'd accept things more readily.

My husband said to me when we were first married, "Don't ever go to sleep being mad. Always kiss good-night." If you kiss good-night, all the troubles break down. No matter how mad you are—and people do have differences of opinion—you basically still like each other.

People are afraid of getting older because they fear they won't be able to do the things they used to. But I don't think that senility necessarily has to accompany old age. There was a time when older people just sat and didn't do much. They dressed "old." I can remember a picture of one of my grandmothers, looking like Whistler's mother. She wore a little cap and a black taffeta dress with a wide round collar covering the shoulders. When people used to be *considered* old, they acted that way.

The young people I know add hope, affection and gaiety to my life.

"Senior citizens"—I hate that term. I think the word "adultery" is better! Anyway, today's older people are not just sitting around waiting to die, *if* they're well.

What bothers me today? Let me think. I get annoyed that we're giving millions to other countries when we have such a need for money right here in some of our cities. I don't understand all these robberies and holdups. I don't think it's only a matter of needing money for dope; I think there's a degeneration in morals and values.

A couple of years ago I was knocked down in the subway

and someone took my bag. It was three o'clock in the afternoon. But that didn't stop me from riding in the subway. It isn't going to happen every day. I don't believe in going through life being afraid of things. I *also* don't believe in sticking your neck out. You just don't do things that ask for trouble.

I don't think older people should impose their own will on younger people. I think, though, you can tell them what you think about things. I'll tell my son and his wife, "Look, this is what I would do. But if you want to do it differently, it's all right with me."

The young can give the old kindness and understanding. They don't have to make them feel as if they're old fuddy-duddies. I think the majority of young people today are absolutely fabulous. The ones I know add hope, affection and gaiety to my life.

Fran Lee

CONSUMER ACTIVIST

She is a frequent guest on television talk shows because of her flamboyant dress and her outspoken candor on controversial subjects. Fran Lee Weiss, sixty-nine, speaks out against injustice, government deception and corporate irresponsibility.

As a consumer activist, a meticulous and thorough researcher, she is determined to inform the public about frauds, deceptive advertising and dangers to health. Honored for "fearless reporting," she has pursued her charges of corruption on the lecture circuit, in print and on the television and radio. Sometimes she has sought legal redress by suing the Parks Department, the Board of Health, the Police Department, the mayor and others. She is the founder and cochairperson of Children Before Dogs, a nonprofit organization devoted to protecting children and adults against the dangers of dog diseases.

She has played dramatic parts in more than six hundred shows, including *Medea* with John Gielgud and Judith Anderson and *Anna Lucasta* with Kim Stanley. She has acted in more than five hundred commercials. And in the role of "Mrs. Fixit," in a nightly news spot, she has demonstrated hundreds of money-saving ideas to television audiences across the country.

When she welcomes me to her apartment, she is wearing a geometrically printed caftan of white, black and brown. She insists first on a tour of her four and a half rooms. The apartment is crowded with art and knick-knacks that she and her husband of fifty years, Sam Weiss, a retired tax attorney, have collected on their visits to more than ninety countries. On the closet doors, running the length of a wall and facing the twin beds, is a mural of the ocean. "Sam promised me we'd live on the water," she explains with a smile.

Fran Lee is a handsome woman with a new look. She's recently had her silver-white hair transformed into what she calls a "Jewish Afro." She's traded in her rhine-stone-studded glasses for a pair with large, rose-tinted frames.

Fran and I sit on white leather furniture in the living room. She talks fast. "I'm not ulcerous," she claims. "I'm vital." Her thoughts tumble out as one word or phrase reminds her of something else.

She's not afraid to name names as she cites personalities and corporations who've earned her wrath. And to guarantee I will be faithful to her words, she tape-records me taping her.

Fran is highly emotional. Tears fill her eyes as she recalls battles fought over the years. Her alto voice vibrates with passion. She describes herself as "extreme, flamboyant and colorful." And she is.

*Y*ou will work out, you won't rust out." That's a personal conviction or theory I have. I get up anywhere from six-thirty to nine, arthritic. I let Sammy sleep. I go into the den and shut the door. I work in so many areas that I need time to organize my life, so those few hours are precious. I take my tea and I clean up from the night before.

I turn on the news and I see things that are wrong. This is a lousy world. Just look at the headlines. Well, a minute later I'm on the phone and I'm raising hell! They know it's Fran Lee—no anonymous calls! By eleven, the activity creates activity. The arthritis is there but it's forgotten. The blood is hot.

I'm one of the few reporters who's a member of the New York Academy of Sciences. I have the ability to feed back in simple language the things I find fascinating. I'm a thorough medical researcher. I did the first exposé on cyclamates, cold-water humidifiers, swine flu. I did the first story on microwave-oven damage. I've told the cosmetic industry that what they're selling are not jars of hope, but jars of hoax. I ask for responsibility in manufacturing— that ads be filled with truth instead of deceit.

You're stuck with a faulty product? Whether it's one rotten strawberry or a broken zipper, *take it back!* And either get on the phone or write nasty letters to the president of the company. Make your complaint known.

In my opinion, the people who promote products, who do the commercials—and who haven't tested the products and don't know what they're talking about—are whores. Sure, I'd like to endorse something for a lot of money. But it would have to be some product I've researched and found healthy and safe.

I've walked off shows where they've wanted me to pimp. They've offered me money under the table to sell things I don't believe in. I won't. I can't compromise. What sustains me is knowing I'm right.

I was brought up as a pacifist but now I'm a fighter. If I have to use my fists today, I will. Now I would carry a gun. I'd carry it for Israel. I'd carry it for kids, who are at the bottom of our list of priorities. When I spoke out against child abuse, referring to dogs that were better fed, I was booed. I got death threats. We had to call the FBI.

I turn on the morning news and I see things that are wrong. Well, a minute later I'm on the phone raising hell.

After my experience with the court system, I don't believe in waiting for them to solve things. Take last night's television drama on rape. If I had been the mother of that girl, believe me, that rapist would have been dead. I probably would have knifed him in the genitals or shot him full of holes.

I've developed a temper over the years about the unjust war in Vietnam, where we killed youth for nothing. Who says *they* can kill, but *I* can't—for a just cause.

I don't know about capital punishment. And yet I don't want to pay for a murderer sitting up there. The reasons would have to be enormous for me to mete out punishment to a stranger. Yet I believe in an eye for an eye—in anything that touched me or those I loved. I could kill for *my* family, yet I don't know whether I approve of capital punishment.

Even before there was women's lib, Sammy let me be me. He always says, "I plucked a rose and got the thorn." It's been a strange marriage. He's my complete opposite in temperament. I met him at a dance when I was fifteen. He was twenty-one. He was the kind of boy I didn't like. He wore glasses—the typical Jewish accountant type. He was my first boyfriend. I was an innocent with long curls. I was so shy and self-conscious about the freckle on my nose that I used to talk to people with my head down.

We were virgins. I thought you got pregnant if you kissed on the lips. We were married in a synagogue near here. On our wedding night I heard him in the bathroom washing his face and brushing his teeth, and I got scared. I didn't like the way it sounded. I got into my little black suit and just started crying. He came out and rocked me in his arms the entire night. He must have been pretty hot in the pants but he didn't touch me.

Well, we adjusted to each other, physically, mentally, emotionally.

I say, "Talk it out. Cry it out." I had to teach my husband to yell and cry. Then you know where you stand. When couples say they never argue, that's bullshit. If you love each other, you've got to argue. Who could be with a person day in and day out and *not?*

I believe in sticking with a marriage unless the guy is a rapist, a drunk or he beats you. Then walk! But for everything else, the little incompatibilities, you can make a go of it.

When Sammy used to come home from law school, I'd be washing and boiling diapers. He'd say, "Let's do it together, Fran. We'll get done quicker." He vacuums. He wallpapered part of this apartment. We're a team.

I joined the women's movement right away. I was excited. But I'm good at smelling rot. And there's something about the leaders that wasn't middle America, and that's why they lost. They looked down their noses at families, at women with children and grandchildren. Those broads don't know what a team is.

If you love each other, you've got to argue. Who could be with a person day in and day out and not?

Open up *Ms.* magazine. You'll see ten ads for liquor and cigarettes. I wrote them right away: "You know babies are born slow, thin. You know women shouldn't smoke. We're getting as dumb as the men. Is this an example?" They never answered me.

Physically, I'm a strong woman. Both Sammy and I have low blood pressure, low cholesterol. We eat all the butter and eggs that we want. Genetically, we're lucky.

I'm *for* estrogen. I'm a postmenopausal woman who wouldn't be talking to you today if I didn't take estrogen for fifteen years. I was forty-eight when I began my change of life. If you're an emotional young woman, you become a doubly emotional menopausal woman. I used to sit here with perspiration dripping off me. I forgot where I went to buy bread. One day Sammy came home and found me sitting in the closet.

Nature just cuts you off. Forget the bunch that say menopause is *just* in your mind! I know it's not.

The only good thing about menopause is: no more periods, no more walking with a rag that chafes you. Don't forget I come from the era where there were no tampons. And there's no more worrying about getting pregnant. My husband always used condoms. He would never allow me to use the Pill and harm my body just so that he could get his pleasure.

I had my kids when I wanted them. I had them when I could afford them. And I didn't destroy a man who was trying to make a living, by having eight or ten kids. I had two. I used common sense.

I'm a constructive lady who says, "Use your hands. Don't smoke. Substitute. Wash the bathroom floor." We used to have a cleaning lady once a week, but no more. We figured out that, since Sam's retired, the money we save is enough for a round-trip ticket to Africa.

I don't believe in psychiatrists. If you're depressed, I believe you should push the furniture and scrub the floor. Put the money in the bank you'd pay for a psychiatrist and get on with life!

I think it's important to give yourself a change of pace. I come home and do the exact opposite of what I've been doing. I drop the pocketbook, the briefcase, and I read something that has nothing to do with what I've been out lecturing about. I'll say to Sammy, "No eating in tonight. We'll go out, have a cheap meal, see a movie." Two hours out of the house and we're back. If I don't do it, I find myself getting tighter and tighter.

Changing pace has saved my life. Also hot baths. When I couldn't afford perfume, I'd put a few drops of vanilla in the bath water.

I like to "give myself a rose." An old lady years ago said to me, "You should have a porcelain cup. I know you love tea. That cup is only yours. You can't afford to go out; you can't go to the beauty parlor. Sit down away from the family and have your tea in a porcelain cup." Well, that old English lady gave me one as a gift. It was so delicate. The family knew no one was to touch it but me. That's giving myself a rose—learning to love myself. The porcelain cup, the hot baths, a little rouge, a little lipstick, two drops of perfume behind the ears—it's so simple. When you love yourself, people will love you.

I'm not scared when I have to address a large audience or appear on television. An actress once said to me before an audition, "Just picture everyone taking down their pants and going to the toilet exactly like you do." I say to myself, "I am beautiful. I am loved. And I have a secret. If you could do better, you'd be up here where I am."

I don't believe in psychiatrists. Put the money in the bank and get on with life!

I was on the "Tomorrow" show. My topic was: "Oral sex causes blindness due to herpes simplex." NBC fell on the floor. The censors went crazy. My mail was incredible. I'm a prude; I'd never practice oral sex. I don't think God intended a penis to go in someone's mouth. Nature didn't make a penis to be used as a lollipop.

I've never approved of my language. But I think as you get older you can be as outrageous as you wish. I use words as a punch in the nose. I want to get your attention. I want you to listen to me. If you won't listen when I say "poo-poo," "do-do," "excrement," then I'll say "shit." Why are we so caught up in "bad" words while our world is dying?

I know I'm naughty. I do these things to provoke. I believe in stimulation. Make them think! Get them mad! Get the adrenaline going!

I've always been different. I had too much strength; I stuck out like a sore thumb. Sammy used to call me his "steel marshmallow." You didn't think it when you first met me. I was gentle and lovely. But then I'd open my mouth, and all hell would break out.

I get up every day and know I'm going to get bruised. The majority of people have a "Don't rock the boat" philosophy. Well, I can't accept that. I see life as a crooked picture and I want to straighten it. I want the world to be nice.

Sammy and I have a pact. We're against cemeteries of all kinds. We belong to a society that will take us from wherever we die immediately to a crematorium. I believe you should talk to me and love me in life. Don't say a word over me in death.

I've told my sons that I don't want one nickel spent on a synagogue or a funeral of any kind. It's in my will. Sammy and I would like to die together, in a plane. We don't want tubes, no prolonging of life. We want to go in dignity. This is my body, my life. Who gives you the right to interfere, to prolong my life? I don't want to be paralyzed. I don't want to be blind. I want to go fast. Let me die in an accident, with my Sammy, quick.

I remember being on a plane, coming back from Poland. It was 1970. They said, "Take off your glasses and your shoes. We're coming down in a field. Throw everything in the blanket as the stewardess comes by." I didn't cry. I sat quietly. I was only angry that Sam wasn't with me.

*I see life as a crooked picture and I want
to straighten it.*

Older people have clout now. Maggie Kuhn calls herself
a Gray Panther. I think of myself as a White Tiger. We're
on the same side.

Some older people are frightened, vulnerable, locked
into their tiny room. On every single block there should
be a meeting space, a room, where older people could
congregate. There'd be crafts, cards, games. Young people would come, too. The government should pay for this.

You go to a mechanic to fix your car. That makes sense.
For help with a difficult recipe, you wouldn't go to a mechanic; you'd go to a cook. So why can't grandparents and
older people be the cooks of wisdom? I've lived a certain
number of years. I must have learned something.

Grace Chu

COOKING TEACHER, AUTHOR

To the right of the apartment door hangs a six-inch bar with Chinese characters. The red background is for good luck. The gold-colored characters signify "Chu Residence."

Madame Grace Zia Chu is five feet tall and, she says, "a little chubby." (*Madame* was a title first used when her husband was in the diplomatic corps.)

She is eighty years old. With her full face and silver-rimmed glasses, she looks like a spectacled cherub. Her face is bare of make-up. Her black hair is cut short. She wears black pants, a multicolored shirt, black velvet flat shoes and a watch on a chain around her neck. She keeps track of the time, mindful of her weekly appointment at a nearby beauty parlor.

Madame Chu has been teaching Americans about Chinese food for a quarter of a century. She founded the course in Chinese cooking at the China Institute in New York City. She has demonstrated her techniques and taught classes in department stores, churches, hotels and on the ship *Queen Elizabeth II.* Currently she teaches cooking in her own home.

The kitchen, to my eye, is surprisingly small. Classes are conducted in the dining room. The students work on an expandable bridge table. They consume the completed meal at Madame Chu's dining-room table.

Madame Chu has been a consultant on five cookbooks. She is the author of *The Pleasures of Chinese Cooking* and *Madame Chu's Chinese Cooking School.* She finds French cooking "too rich and complicated." Her favorite American food is steak.

We talk in the living room of the three-bedroom co-operative apartment.

My father died when I was sixteen. My mother died two years later. I was the oldest of eight children.

My father was a Christian religious writer and a scholar. He edited the Y.M.C.A. magazine for China. He was a very strong, outspoken man. He made decisions quickly. He died of tuberculosis caused, I think, by overwork. My mother didn't do anything professionally. When she graduated from high school she married my father. She was a quiet woman.

I got a scholarship to go to America. That was God's gift to me. Physical education was my major. I graduated from Wellesley College in 1924 and got my certificate in hygiene and physical education in 1925. It was a very complicated course. You had to know all about anatomy and physiology.

Then I went back to China. I taught first in the high school where I had been a student and then in Ginling College in Nanking. In Ginling, I taught physical-education teachers how to teach.

When I was young, by American standards of physical education I wasn't quite an expert. But compared to Chinese ladies, who were quiet, serious, sedate, I was very active. I was considered an extrovert.

My husband and I met while we were both studying near Boston. He graduated from M.I.T. We were completely different in personality. He was very quiet, an introvert. He was always suspicious of people. He was too cautious for me.

Today, students don't go back to China to live. In the old days, the students went back because they wanted to work in their own country. My husband and I went back. He became a military attaché to the Chinese Embassy in Moscow and Washington. We did quite a lot of traveling with our two sons while they were growing up. When the war came, when the situation was no longer stable, we left China. I became an American citizen in 1955.

Americans, because they're affluent, overeat. Chinese people don't have enough money to eat junk food.

My husband has been dead almost twenty years. I never wanted to remarry. I became very interested in having a profession.

My husband didn't leave me much money. I've always been self-employed, so I have no pension. I only have Social Security. My two sons, ever since they've earned a living, have given me a check every month. They do it willingly and happily. For Chinese, it's good because you save face. People say I've trained my sons well.

The cooking started when I was fifty-five. I needed to make a living. I was wondering whether to take a refresher course in physical education. I had been away from it for almost twenty years. Did I want to spend more time and money, and then maybe not be able to get a job? Was it worthwhile at my age to go back to a profession which really requires youth? If not, then I'd have to find myself a different job. Those were things going through my mind.

I like people. And the people I liked I cooked for. It's not because I was an expert, that I knew so much about cooking. I didn't. But I was Chinese. I cooked Chinese. I knew the nuance of Chinese cooking.

I started to cook for my friends. They said, "Why don't you teach us?" Although I had learned teaching methods, I didn't think I could teach cooking. I was used to cooking with my eyes, my ears, my head. I cooked by instinct. Yet when you *teach* cooking you have to be very exact.

So I tried a few dishes. In the beginning it was very hard to be so scientific. But people seemed to like me and my classes.

I began to teach teachers. That I liked. That's how I'm different. I think I'm the only one in the United States who has trained a group of Americans to be teachers of Chinese cooking.

The classes grew through word of mouth. People wanted to learn from Madame Chu. The classes grew to thirty students. That was no good, I thought, because it became a demonstration, not a class. So I refused to teach large groups.

I like to work. But as people get older I think they should taper off in their work and enjoy life as well. I used to teach six classes a week. This year I'm going to teach only one group of five sessions. Then I'll decide whether to do more.

Chinese food is very healthy. It's not heavy. It has less calories because we use vegetable oil. It's low in cholesterol. And it's economical because we use small amounts of meat. Americans, because they're affluent, overeat. Chinese people don't have enough money to eat junk food.

I like to train teachers because then I know my work is being carried on. I'm not jealous of other teachers. Being realistic, how can I possibly do everything myself? I want more people to learn about cooking. And the world is so large. There is enough Chinese food for everyone to eat and to learn how to prepare. I'm not afraid that someone will steal one of my dishes. You can take my exact recipes and everything I do, but it will be different. The personality of the teacher is important.

When I hear someone has an interest in teaching, I tell them to come and be my assistant, for free. And when they're on their own, if they have a problem, they'll call me.

The family system held China together. American society does not respect the family to the same degree.

I have very good students. I think nice of them, they think nice of me. But after they leave, I'm only hoping they're cooking Chinese. I am a Chinese educated in America. I make my life here. So it's my duty to promote the cultural relationship between the two countries. Chinese cooking is so popular now that I feel my mission is accomplished.

I have one son who lives in the city. I don't see him that often, about twice a month. In between, we talk on the phone. He married a lovely American girl three years ago. I'm very fond of her. She consults me about a number of different things. She asks my opinion, so I feel very honored.

The other son has three children; the oldest one is at Yale. My son's wife is Chinese; she teaches piano. I like her too. But they live in another state.

I don't want to annoy them or interfere in their lives. I am a strong person; I know that about myself. I sometimes offend people by my fast way of saying what I think. Yet I do not mean to hurt them.

If your daughter-in-law's not close to you, I think it's the fault of your son. Your daughter-in-law never knew you before she married your son. The son might have said, "My mother is so bossy. Play along with her." And she thinks, "Oh, that's the attitude to have." So then the scene is set. It's worse if your son does not respect you. He might say, "My mother never had an education," or, "My mother's spoiled." Then the daughter-in-law has that same impression.

When my sons were growing up they thought I was perfect. They'd think, "If my mother were here, things would be different." But now that's changed. They're my worst critics. And I'm glad. If they still thought I was perfect, it would mean they wore blinders, that they had no mind of their own.

The family system has held China together. American society does not respect the family to the same degree. I think young people today are being raised too permissively. It's the fault of Dr. Spock. Many parents, college graduates, don't want to take the trouble to provide discipline and guidance. Giving children money is not enough. Why are there so many Moonies? Why did so many people go to Jonestown, Guyana? They were looking for something.

Parents should not live with their married children. The best thing is to live in the same city. Sometimes children are very busy. I think then you become a burden; they feel guilty because they're good children and they *want* to see you, but they don't have the time. It's understandable. But it's not very nice to have a situation where their conscience always bothers them. And if they're *not* good children, then you feel bad not to see them when they're so near.

I don't call my son in New York regularly. Some American mothers I know call Tuesday, Thursday and Sunday mornings at ten. And they have nothing interesting to say. Sometimes I'll call two times, maybe more. But there's no schedule. Sometimes a whole week can go by when I'm busy, so I don't call. Eventually we catch up.

I used to think you look for happiness. Now I've decided you make and create your own.

I don't like to get up early. Unless I have something special to do, I'll usually get up around eight, eight-fifteen. It takes around an hour for me to wake up. I read the *Times* every day; that's important to me since I don't watch much television or listen to the radio. Then I'll do whatever chores are needed around the house.

A few students in each class have become my friends, mostly Americans. We'll meet for lunch or dinner or go to a concert. I take a short nap every afternoon. I had double pneumonia in 1971. It was very serious; I had to rest for a whole year.

I think I work best after dinner. From about eight to twelve, I write letters and articles. I listen to music, to opera. I read books in both Chinese and English. Maybe I'll watch something on public television, the station without the commercials. Yet most of the time I feel too active to sit down and watch it.

I like to play mah-jong with four friends. I also have several groups I play with in the vicinity. The game may start in the afternoon and last until the evening. If they play here, I make dinner. This hobby is important to me. One has to have a group of friends. I get to sleep about one, one-thirty. That's why I sleep late in the morning.

One thing that American society lacks, from my point of view, is that people don't have *groups* of friends. You have one individual friend. And if something happens to him or her, you have no one to talk to. And you wind up at the psychiatrist's. I think you have to have people you can depend on. I have friends who let me talk things out. Through the talking, I realize what I must do.

I say what I need to say and I sleep peacefully. I don't pretend. I don't scheme. If someone criticizes me, why should I take it seriously? If she meant to make me unhappy, and I cry and lose sleep—well, that's what she wanted. I'm not going to let her have the pleasure.

So you may occasionally fight with your friends, but in the end you still have people to count on. This society is breaking down because it's just one-to-one. And when you get married it seems you give up all your old friends. So what happens if you get a divorce?

I used to think you *look* for happiness. Now I've decided you make and create your own. When *you're* happy, other people feel good too. Don't be woebegone and sad. Don't fuss so much over yourself. It's been two years since I've used cosmetics. I never wore that much—just a little lipstick, a little rouge. Now I don't even own any. And I don't miss it. I said, "It's a nuisance. I don't need it."

Learn to think *less* of yourself and more of others. If you're affluent, then you should give money to other people. If you're not so rich but you have a little more energy, then you should give of yourself in other ways. I might help someone who has trouble walking to get on the bus. It's the little things we do for each other that count. And gradually you become used to helping people.

I talk to the cashiers in the supermarket. Sometimes they look very grouchy. I'll say, "Good morning. You've been very busy this morning, huh?" Well, then they smile. If you can get someone to smile, then you've given them a little happiness. And it cost you nothing. The more you give, the more you're happy and then there's no time for loneliness.

At my age, my immediate memory has failed. The early memory is all right. I used to be able to read a book and remember what it was all about. Now I read one and enjoy it, and two weeks later the details escape me. I also have trouble remembering people's names. I'll know the face and where we met, but the person's name just floats away.

If I stay with older people, not old in age but old in activity, then I get fretful. I need to be active.

I don't hide my age. I don't sit here and moan, "Oh, dear, now I'm eighty." I rather enjoy it. The Chinese like to be older. There's respect for older people. So if you were to go to China and say you were eighty, you could probably do many things you couldn't do here.

The Chinese people go on protocol. Old ladies sit down before the young ones. Old ladies leave a room before the young. Sometimes that bothers me because I'm impatient. "After you." "No, after you." Well, that's a waste of time. I guess now I have a combination of the American and the Chinese in me.

Just because I'm eighty, I'm not an old lady. I just do less.

I think people should face old age. They should talk about it, plan for it. Lots of people say, "Don't talk about it. I'm not there yet." Just because I'm eighty, I'm not an old lady. I just do less. I used to do three, four, five things at the same time. I don't anymore.

Age has nothing to do with sex. You don't say, "I'm forty years old, I'm sixty years old, I'm eighty, so don't touch me !" You don't give up sex. I think it has more to do with desire. I know plenty of young people who marry and have a good life, yet sex isn't a major part of their relationship.

I never felt curtailed. I never felt unliberated. But in this country, where law is everything, women have to fight for equality. Yet my personality is such that I never want to be number one. Number one shoulders all the blame and all the responsibility. I'd rather not be the president of the United States. I'd rather be the vice-president.

Women can do everything that men can do and one thing more. They can bear children. In China, women are latecomers. But now it's easier for them to move up. Women have the opportunity to be anything.

I'm sorry to say that I'm not a very formal religious person. I'm not the type who says grace at every meal, who kneels down in prayer, who goes to church every week. I wish I was. Maybe when I get older! I believe strongly in God and in his guidance. Oftentimes, either late at night or in the morning before I get up, I say, "Thank you, Lord, for another night. Let me get up and do something to make someone happy in my little way." I try to live Christianity. I aim at doing something good for mankind, not necessarily for one church.

I believe in capital punishment. Isn't that sad? But I think *no* capital punishment is even worse.

I have made a will. I have listed the people I want to get my mementos: this ring goes to . . . this pin to so-and-so. I want no memorial service, no one to sing my praises. I have been to so many services for people who really haven't done much. They lived, raised a family and died. Everybody does that. After you're dead, people who didn't like you have to say nice things about you. That's dishonest.

I wanted my ashes to be dropped from the Staten Island ferry in the middle of the night. But then I thought, "Oh, dear, that's pollution!" So my older son thought of something else. Now, after I die, someone will take my ashes, on a rainy day like today, and drive along the highway. They can drop my ashes along the bank of the road, where the trees will grow and grow.

It's a burden for someone to go and visit ashes in an urn or a grave in a cemetery. If they don't go, their conscience will bother them. If they do go, they just waste time. And what do they do when they get there? Just stand and stare? If they remember you, they remember you.

I don't want anyone passing the hat on my behalf. But

I'm in favor of education. If someone wants to take *their* money and start a scholarship in my name, as a memorial, that's okay.

I want to be happy and useful. In my own way, I think I'm doing that.

Helene Papanek

PSYCHIATRIST

Dr. Helene Papanek was born in Vienna in 1901. For the past thirty years she has lived in Manhattan. Her comfortable home is a large, airy, seven-room apartment. There's a magnificent view of the city from her office and living room.

Dr. Papanek, a widow for nine years, the mother of two sons, at the age of seventy-eight still maintains a private practice in psychiatry. She is executive director emeritus of the Alfred Adler Institute, where she did her postdoctoral psychiatric training and was the executive director for twenty-seven years. She continues to supervise students and participates in an advisory capacity in the administration of the institute.

Dr. Papanek is a gray-haired, motherly looking woman. Her height used to be five feet, two inches; but she has shrunk an inch with age. Her baby-blue dress brings out the blue in her eyes. She wears terry-cloth espadrilles of red, white and blue.

Her office, where we talk, is bathed in sunlight. There are a couch, two armchairs and a working fireplace. Dr.

Papanek sits behind her paper-strewn desk. On the wall behind her are medical diplomas and awards.

Dr. Papanek's voice is strong, the words tinged with a Viennese accent.

Although I was born in Vienna, my parents were Russian Jews. My mother came to Vienna to study economics. That was unusual for a woman. But she never had a profession. She married my father and had four children. My parents were middle class; we were very comfortable.

My father was a doctor and owned a sanitorium, a private hospital in Vienna. My father wanted someone in the family to take over. My younger brother didn't want to be a doctor, so it was up to me.

In high school, I always liked animals and plants. I had a collection of insects and a herbarium. When I was fourteen, fifteen, I read Darwin and other scientific books. At eighteen I started studying medicine. That may seem early, but it was a normal age for middle Europe.

I became friendly with my husband in 1918. We were engaged for seven years. We had sex before we were married. My mother did her best to keep us apart; she was quite Victorian.

My father didn't want me to get married. Perhaps he thought I wouldn't continue with my work. He made me promise not to marry before I finished medical school. So I married two days after I graduated.

In Vienna I worked with men all the time. When I was in training I used to perform autopsies with five men. I didn't like the jokes they made all the time. I didn't like their eating sandwiches at the dissecting table. But I got used to it all.

I had one professor who I'm sure asked me certain questions just to embarrass me. He was also responsible for the city of Vienna's hospitals. He got me a job in a hospital for incurables. Incurables are interesting medically, but I was responsible for thousands of patients. I always had the feeling that this professor deliberately gave me this appointment because I was a married woman.

I don't think everyone can benefit from therapy. A patient has to want *to change.*

In the early days my husband was a politician, a social democrat. He was the youngest member of the Diet of Vienna. It ended in 1934 with the coming of fascism. My husband left for France. I stayed with our two children and continued my work. But in 1938 Hitler took over Austria. So we left too.

We were reunited as a family in Paris. With the collapse of France we came by boat to America on visitors' visas. My husband became the director of the Wiltwyck School, a rehabilitation center for boys. He was also a professor at Queens College.

I took the national medical-board examinations and spent a year interning in the Bronx. At the time, we lived in Queens. We didn't have much money. My older son was drafted and shipped to Europe, where he became a translator for prisoners of war. My younger son got a scholarship to private school.

I opened an office in Queens as a general practitioner. I began to feel that half the patients who came to see me had psychosomatic diseases. It was frustrating to try to practice medicine when so many patients were just suffering from unhappiness and dissatisfaction.

I felt I was very sensitive to emotional problems. I know I'm intelligent. So I took additional training at the Postgraduate Center for Mental Health. Then I rented an office in Manhattan to do psychotherapy. I drove back and forth between that office and my general practice in Queens.

I'm an Adlerian-trained therapist. I couldn't stomach Freud's ideas of sex. Adlerian therapy was an alternative to Freudianism and behaviorism; it's a humanistic approach. Adlerian therapists believe that man's behavior is not determined by biological instincts and inner drives, nor by stimulation from the outside. Rather, it is determined by what Adler called the creative power of the individual directed toward functioning as a positive member of society.

In my practice I see more women than men. More younger people than ever before are seeking some sort of psychiatric help. People come to therapy because something bothers them. I have a very successful career woman who's been with me for five years. She's a lesbian. She said that the best thing I did for her was to "permit" her to live with her female lover. But she's now afraid of losing her job.

My patients sit up in a chair. I want them to have a real relationship with me, not a fantasy. Sitting behind the patient increases the fantasy because the doctor is anonymous.

I don't have a secret power to make people feel better. They come here because they have flaws. They learn to accept their flaws because I like them as people, in spite of the flaws. They might be overly ambitious, overly compulsive, overly selfish, overly insecure. Then we work together. They begin to accept the shortcomings which have made them lonely and dissatisfied.

I don't think everyone can benefit from therapy. A patient first has to be able to admit that something is wrong. Then they have to *want* to change.

You can find a therapist by recommendation of a friend; or by looking in the Yellow Pages under "Psychiatrist"; or by calling a hospital or mental-health clinic for a referral. You can also choose to see a clinical psychologist or a psychiatric social worker. It depends on the person who is best suited for *you*. A therapy "hour" is usually fifty minutes. The rate varies. Seeing someone in a clinic is usually less expensive than going to a private therapist.

I've been lucky. I haven't been forced to retire. I don't feel diminished because I'm older. But old age presents problems.

I don't agree with the women's movement as far as children are concerned. I usually tell my patients they might have to interrupt their lives, their careers, to take care of their children. It might take from one to three years.

I have nothing against a woman having children without a man. I do think, though, it's better if there's a family. I feel the family structure is very important.

When people live together they have to help each other. In spite of differences, there can be equality. My husband did everything but make beds. When we came here our boys were nine and sixteen. They were very responsible children. My husband and sons all washed dishes. They helped out any way they could.

The women's movement has done more good than bad things. Yet I think they exaggerate some things. I believe men and women are different. I believe there are male traits and female traits. I think females are more emotional. I feel that my intelligence is equal to a male's intelligence; I never had difficulty with my studies. And the emotional life didn't have to interfere.

I've been lucky. I haven't been forced to retire. I haven't been ignored. I don't feel diminished because I'm older.

Old age does present some problems. My legs are not as good. I can't walk as long and as far. I cannot carry heavy things. I'm not as strong. But I'm taking driving lessons now, a refresher course. I didn't drive for nine years. I decided that being without a car handicaps me too much.

I get great pleasure in going to museums. I'm sorry that I didn't take drawing lessons. I'd like to be able to draw what I see out my window. It's too difficult for me to learn now.

I've been fortunate. I have enough money so that I don't have to work. I can afford to have a maid, who comes in seven hours a day. I'd like to write my autobiography. I want to write some articles for professional journals.

I have a small practice now. I see only seven patients a week. I can treat people only if I like them. And I like fewer people! Now their complaints get on my nerves. The work is very repetitive. My memory is not as good as it was. I get tired quickly. I'm often irritable, cranky. I'm quick to anger, and that's not good in my profession.

My children wouldn't want me to live with them, even if I wanted to—not even for a night. My older son has a room downstairs in his house that's not in use. It was his daughter's when she was growing up. He feels I wouldn't get along with his wife.

My younger son is divorced. He's too busy having girls in. He doesn't say it, but that's why he doesn't want me to live with him.

If I didn't have money, then I'd expect them to do something for me. We gave to them—all the money for school, for graduate work and afterwards to buy houses. I think they'd owe it back if I needed it. But, now, I don't think they owe me anything. I feel I brought them up well. They respect me. That's different from obligation.

I don't want to live alone all the time. I'm thinking of a retirement home run by the Quakers. It's in the country. There'd be people around. Perhaps I could do some work, something to do with group interaction. Work gives me a lift. I think that's true for everyone.

There's plenty of volunteer work and part-time employment available. If necessary, if people are lonely, they should *force* themselves to get out of the house and do something.

I believe in euthanasia for myself, and I'd do it for someone else. I already have. I think all doctors do it.

My husband was seventy-three when he died. He'd been sick a long time. He had a stroke. He started speaking German to people who didn't understand the language. He wanted to go to Vienna. At the time my brother was in charge of our father's sanitorium. Funny how things work out!

I took my husband to the sanitorium in Vienna where he died. I didn't cry when he died. Today the sanitorium is no longer in our family. It was sold to the city of Vienna.

I have a will. I want to be cremated. I don't care what they do with my ashes or what they say about me.

I'm fearful of dying. I'm afraid of being sick, of being in bed, of not being able to do things for myself. To be dependent on a nurse—that would be terrible.

If I didn't enjoy life anymore, I would consider suicide. I'd take pills. I believe in euthanasia for myself, and I'd do it for someone else. I already have. When I was in Vienna I had a patient with tuberculosis of the larynx. She was in a great deal of pain. I gave her morphine. She said, "Thank you." She knew that after the injection she'd go to sleep without pain. She'd die anyway. I just helped her along.

I think all doctors do it. They just don't tell. For a cancer patient, they give more and more morphine. That kills the patient quicker than a natural death.

Capital punishment is another form of killing. I think it's

cruel and inhuman. I'm against it. It's not a deterrent; people don't *know* why they kill, why they murder.

Enough talk of killing! I'm grateful to be seventy-eight and still functioning. My greatest satisfaction comes in developing a relationship with my patients and helping them work out their problems.

Rose Gale

RETIREMENT HOME RESIDENT

One of the greatest concerns of older Americans is where they will live during their remaining years. A considerable number of them, out of loneliness or physical need, have chosen retirement homes. One of the most pleasant and best run is located on the Upper West Side of Manhattan.

You enter through a double set of glass doors. The security is provided by a buzzer system wired to the second door. It's controlled by the desk clerk, in a glass booth opposite the entrance, who doubles as telephone operator.

The small lobby is tiled in gray-and-white linoleum. Darker gray vertical blinds cover the windows. There are four armchairs and a coffee table. A number of large plants add color.

Past the lobby is the dining room. Clean and stark, it looks like a large coffee shop minus the counter. An announcement makes clear that meals are served at 8:15, at 12:15 and at 5:15. Snacks are available from 3:00 to 4:00, and from 8:00 to 9:00 in the evening.

The spacious mezzanine lounge contains many red couches and armchairs. Religious services and holiday events take place here, as well as recreational activities: mah-jong, arts and crafts, bingo, word games, concerts, movies and discussion groups.

Two elevators carry residents to their single or double rooms. Each guest floor has a small sitting area with a card table, chairs and a television set suspended from the ceiling. Waist-high handrails line the halls.

A single room with private bath costs from $780 to $980 a month. This sum covers the three meals and two snacks daily, as well as maid service. A social worker and an activities director are in daily attendance. A doctor is on call. The rooms are identically furnished. Residents may supply such personal belongings as pictures and photographs, television, radio, books and plants.

The roof, covered with artificial grass, is used during the summer months. There are redwood picnic tables and lounge chairs.

I interview Rose Gale, a seventy-year-old widow, in her private room on the ninth floor. The activities director has told me that Rose is "a joy, runs the whole place, into everything." She is a small, sturdy-looking woman. She wears her short, straight auburn hair pinned behind her ears. Bangs fall halfway down her forehead.

She sits on her single bed, her hand-held crutches resting against the wall. There is a heavy metal brace on her left leg. She is dressed in pale-blue, lightweight slacks, striped T-shirt, turquoise necklace, matching earrings and a utilitarian, black-banded watch. Her rouged face makes her look as if she has just returned from some outdoor activity. She is intense, vibrantly alive, her sparkling blue eyes framed by darkened lashes.

My mother must have been around twenty-one or twenty-two when I was born. I was bright, lovely, full of life, the first child. When I was eight months old I was diagnosed as having polio. For four years my mother carried me around from one hospital to another, from one doctor to another. I didn't walk until I was five, and then it was with braces. The first time I used them, my mother wanted to put them on me, and I wouldn't let her. I remember this quite vividly.

Apparently I was a very independent child. Everything I wanted to do she allowed me to do. She didn't pamper me physically because I was handicapped. There must have been many, many times when I went places by myself—on the subway, in the streetcars, without any escort—that must have given her quite a hard time. Yet she never said, "No, you can't go" or, "I'm afraid for you" or, "I don't think you'll be able to manage it." She never held me back.

I was very strong-willed, and she must have had a very difficult time letting me go my own way. I've admired many women, but my mother was my chief role model. She gave me independence.

As I grew, there were bad times when I wished I could run, and dance—be more like other children. But that wasn't to be. Sure, it was depressing. But I think I was born with a cheerful, outgoing disposition. That was a kind of compensation. All through my life I've had people who cared about me, who loved me. Aunts, uncles, cousins, friends, all accepted me for who I was. Maybe my parents spoiled me, gave me more than my brother and sister. But they never made me feel incomplete or unworthy because of my handicap. I had responsibilities, chores, just like other children, and I carried them out.

> *It's important to love and to be loved*
> *whether it's a man-woman, a man-man, a*
> *woman-woman relationship.*

My father was more fearful, more protective. If he had had the chance, out of love for me he would have made me into something pitiful.

He worked in a shoestore. He was a supersalesman who worked from eight o'clock in the morning until eleven o'clock at night, six days a week—no vacations. He was known as a "shoe dog." This was before the unions.

I went to college and was trained to be a Latin teacher. Then the Board of Education wouldn't pass me for a license because of my handicap. I was a college graduate, trained in the humanities—and the Department of Vocational Rehabilitation sent me to secretarial school!

Next I took the exam to be a school secretary, and still they wouldn't pass me. They had me at the downtown office four times to walk up and down the steps, which I can do holding onto the banister. My doctor even wrote them a letter guaranteeing I'd be okay. I really would have liked that job. I'd have a pension now and that would be a help. I've never felt discriminated against because I was a woman or old. But this decision was, I felt, discriminatory.

I've done or can do plenty of things. Some I've liked, some I haven't. I learned to drive in a car specially fitted with hand controls, but I never really enjoyed it. I was always frightened about traveling by myself in the car. What would happen if it broke down? What would I do? Where could I go for help? The car was never a source of help or pleasure.

The most important moment in my life was when I got married to the man I loved. I didn't have a "wedding" wedding. It was during the Depression, and he was teaching at a university for the grand sum of fifteen hundred dollars a year. The college had a rule at the time that an instructor couldn't be married. They were still publishing marriage licenses in New York City newspapers, and we were afraid someone from the college might read our names in the paper.

So one day we just decided to go off and get married in another state. It was a small, quiet ceremony with just our best friends present. They were rich for those days: they had a car! They provided the transportation. The justice of the peace looked like a southern colonel with a long white mustache. He was over six feet tall. I remember him as quite handsome.

I've never in my life been anti-male. Yet I've always been resentful about men who never help women. My husband was an unusual man in that respect. He said he didn't have to prove his masculinity by not washing dishes, by not ironing clothes, by not sewing. He did everything in the household that I did. He never felt ashamed or diminished.

For a long, long time we tried to have a child. Then it happened, and we were delighted. I was forty-one when our daughter was born, and my hair was snowy white. I'd take her to the park every day and sit with all the young-looking mothers in their twenties and thirties. One day a woman asked, "Is she your grandchild?" I don't know why that upset me, but it did. I dyed my hair.

I have some regrets about my daughter. I think I was too strict in demanding certain kinds of behavior from her. With her musical ability, I was very severe about her practicing.

Music is my greatest joy and pleasure. Looking back over my life, I think I could have tried harder to become a professional singer, to be on the concert stage. I had a very beautiful voice and I studied singing, but I didn't have the motivation to spend all those hours practicing. Maybe I was lazy. At the time it was easier not to do it.

But I forced my daughter to practice, sometimes spanking her to make her do it. I'm very sorry for that. She eventually dropped it altogether, I think as a result of my actions.

I didn't want to go into this retirement home. My psychiatrist insisted. I'm glad he did. I would not change back to my former house or former life for anything in the whole world.

I think one of the goals of parenthood would be to live long enough to see your children have an understanding of what you've done in your life for their growth—to understand it even when they resent you, so it no longer colors their feelings about you.

I think children owe something to parents. Perhaps "owing" is the wrong word. I think in any relationship you give and you take. A parent gives when her children are young, and a child takes. And when the children get older, they give joy to the parent, pleasure—and they give pain because they can be such damn nuisances. And parents can be mean and nasty to their kids even when they love them very much. Not everything is a bed of roses either way.

No parent is perfect and no child is perfect. But when you're a parent you are giving all the time and you never stop. You are never, never *not* a parent. Your children are your great concern no matter how old you get. You belong to each other. You're a part of each other.

And yet I wouldn't want to live with my daughter under any circumstances. Our lifestyles are so different that I couldn't live the way she lives for anything in the world.

I'm methodical; she's not. I'm organized; she's surrounded by chaos. I guess I'm rigid.

I'd be lonely if I lived with her. She has her own life to live, which doesn't involve baby-sitting her mama. I wouldn't want to give her the burden of guilt of going out and feeling I'd be there all alone while she was having a good time. We fight and we disagree in so many areas even though we love each other dearly and deeply. But there are also many areas in which we have great rapport, like music and art.

My daughter is single. I'd like her to be happily in love. It's important to love and to be loved whether it's a man-woman, a man-man, a woman-woman relationship. I'd like my daughter to be married but I've never urged her.

Aside from my husband's death, the most traumatic thing that ever happened to me was when my mother died. I was a grown-up woman with a child, but it was still a tremendous blow. I don't care how old you are. You are *left,* and you are then the older generation. When a parent is alive, you're still somebody's child. So when my mother died I took it very hard. She had a heart attack, and by the time I could get to her she was dead.

I'm handy the way she was; I can fix things around the house. I know I inherited her very beautiful voice. We were both emotional, high-strung people. For a few days after she died, I kept dreaming the same dream. I held her in my arms and rocked her, saying, "Oh, Mama, don't be dead." That was eighteen years ago. It was a deep sorrow, and I guess a lasting grief.

For a number of years I was in a deep depression and had to be hospitalized. Perhaps the trigger was my husband's death. I had leaned on him so completely that I fell apart when he died. I kept thinking, "Who will do *this* for me? Who will do *that* for me?"

Although I was an independent person I had never really gone places alone nor been alone for any length of time. And I found I didn't enjoy it. Physically I could have managed, but part of the pleasure was sharing with someone else and that was missing. For the first time in my life I truly felt handicapped. It was an anxiety that tore at my guts.

I remember a feeling of sweet sadness—a kind of remorse. But it went beyond mourning. There was a sense of forlornness that I couldn't shake even when I was having a good time. The feeling would well up inside me. I couldn't function on any level. I would shake and moan. I couldn't eat. I had to force myself to do the simplest kind of thing. I kept repeating and repeating myself until even my best friends couldn't stand me.

Luckily I had a psychiatrist who saw *me* and understood *me* as a person. He felt that what I needed was people. When I had them I was okay. When I was alone I was not.

I didn't want to go into this retirement home. I guess I was scared of giving up my life—my books, my paintings on the wall, my ambience. At my house I was in possession of my life. I couldn't imagine being in a regimented institution. The thought of being with old people all the time bothered me. I fought going into the home for months. I pushed the idea aside.

My psychiatrist insisted. And I'm glad he did. I'm most happy here. I've become what I once was in every way. I'm busy in all kinds of things. I write and edit the newspaper. I participate in the discussion groups, the sing-alongs, the poetry workshop. It's three years now, and I would not change back to my former house or life for anything in the world. I'm a survivor! Here, people think I'm kind of wonderful. Well, that feeds your ego. It makes you bud, it makes you flower, it makes you grow. At least it does me.

My psychiatrist was right for me. He gave me good advice and I'm glad I took it. People have a lot of hang-ups about getting professional help. I think people should go to a psychiatrist or a clinical psychologist when they're in a deep depression, when they have problems they can't solve or cope with by themselves. A family can't always help because they're too intimately involved. You need someone who's outside of you, someone you can relate to who is not a friend.

And, luckily, I am still able to treasure the company of my best friend. She's a widow with two grown children. We have the same interests and philosophy. I love her. With all the moves, changes, ups and downs we've both gone through, we've kept in touch. Now I see her maybe every two weeks or so and we talk on the telephone. During that period when I was mentally ill, when I was so depressed, so impossible as a person, she was one of the few who was there on call, who was there with me, no matter what. That's friendship.

I hate the term "senior citizen." I'd rather be called "aging." Everybody's doing that.

When you hear a strain of music which touches your heart, and you turn to your friend, and you smile at each other—then you know that the other person is feeling the same thing you are. The sharing of a momentary experience is essential to me. That's another example of a kind of friendship, a closeness if you will.

One of the advantages of being in a place like this is that, when I want to be with people, all I have to do is step out of my room. There are always people to see, people to talk to. When I was home by myself I was lonely. Here I'm not.

The management assigns you to a dining-room table. We're six. It's pleasant most of the time. There are two women who are quite nice, but very quiet; a woman with my interests, whom I enjoy; one man who is terribly depressed and never talks; and another woman who is a compulsive talker.

At least we're not fighting all the time. There are some

tables like that, and others where the people won't even look at each other, much less have a conversation. You could be changed to another table, but it might turn out to be worse. The food and service leave much to be desired, but that's part of my life here, and I accept it.

Sometimes I miss the special foods I used to make. I made a delicious pot roast, a Bourguignonne, a crab meat au gratin. On reflection, I guess I miss *having* them more than *making* them.

I'm grateful I have a room of my own with my own bathroom—at least until my money runs out. I have a radio which is inadequate but still lets me listen to good music. I have some books and pictures around that make me happy. I have some of the things that I need to sustain me and nourish me.

A majority of the people here are senile. They're forgetful. They don't know where they are. They are what people fear about growing old. And when you're constantly in this company it can be depressing. But I've gotten used to it.

What appalls me here is the lack of understanding that some old people have for others. Ones who are well may have no feeling or compassion for ones who are senile. They make jokes at the expense of the senile ones. They get angry if the others repeat themselves. If they see someone wandering around, why don't they take the other person to the mezzanine or perhaps back to the person's room? I wish they wouldn't make fun of the old people who are having problems, wouldn't call them stupid— would be more tolerant.

And there are people here who are quite, quite old and quite all right. They're nice-looking, they're active, their minds are alert. You look at them and say, "Well, maybe I can grow older like that." I think my greatest fear is that one day senility will strike me and my mind will go.

I hate the term "senior citizen." It's annoying. Who's a junior citizen? Who's a freshman citizen? I'd rather be called "aging." Everybody's doing that!

I think you should not indulge yourself in the process of growing old. You shouldn't say, "Well, I'm old now. I won't do this. I can't do that." You shouldn't think of yourself in that way. It's never easy to see yourself growing old. But if you take it in your stride, if you try to be alive, interested and vital, I think you grow old less terribly.

I would like outsiders not to have any different view of people who are old from what they have of anybody else— except where there are frailties. If there *are* physical frailties, be sympathetic, be helpful and kind. If there are mental frailties, be compassionate and tender.

Society should have the view that these people are persons with identity. They are not in a class. There are as many different old people as there are young people in every walk of life. Sixty-five is an arbitrary definition that people are old.

The first time I felt old, I was in a dress shop. I guess I was in my early fifties. I've always loathed shopping. It's the one time that I'm depressed about myself. I have difficulty because I'm short, broad in the back, full-breasted and I don't fit into clothes easily. This one time I needed something dressy. I tried on something sleeveless. I lifted my arm. As I lowered it in the fluorescent light, I saw there were wrinkles in my upper arm, near the armpit. I was so shocked and so depressed that I didn't buy anything. I just went home. I found this sudden awareness terribly upsetting.

I see myself looking the way I did as a very young woman. I look in the mirror and I'm surprised that I have wrinkles.

Look, I don't love physical deterioration. I tint my hair and would have a face-lift if I could afford it. Why not? But gradually I guess I've come to accept the wrinkles because there's nothing I can really do about it.

So much depends on a person's health. If you're physically well it's so much easier to cope. One of the ugliest things is the physical ravages of the body as you grow older, even though it may be very slow for some people. Minor ailments you never had before are suddenly there to annoy you. That's the unpleasant part.

I've only used crutches for the past three years. I used a cane before that. Without the crutches I couldn't get around at all. I find that many, many places will provide a wheelchair. If I want to go to a museum, I call beforehand and they meet me at the door with a wheelchair. I can push myself around. I find that everybody is most gracious about opening doors, using the elevator, showing you this, showing you that.

If I found somebody compatible I would want to be sexually active again.

When I go to Carnegie Hall, an usher opens the side door and helps me onto the lift, the kind that sends things up from the basement. Up I go until the lift is level with the orchestra floor. Sure, it's difficult, but to me the live concert is usually worth the effort.

You do what you have to do. If I have to be hoisted up in a freight elevator to where I'm going, so be it.

I used to take public transportation. I can't manage it now. I'm dependent on taxicabs, unfortunately, and that can become quite expensive.

I think sometimes of my death, but I can't imagine myself being dead. I have a burial plot and a will, but I've not talked about this with my daughter. Perhaps I should. I would not want to live without a glimmer of life except for a beating heart. My daughter has a card saying her organs should be donated. I don't want my body mutilated. Do you think that's strange? At my funeral I wonder what they'll say. I sometimes see myself there.

I'd rather talk about life. If I found somebody compatible I would want to be sexually active again. I am everybody's girlfriend here and no one's sweetheart. I do not meet men here whom I would like to go to bed with. Part of it is my physical handicap. Men sort of move away for that reason, which they never did when I was young. I like men to be fond of me, to be affectionate. But in all the years I've been widowed, I've never met one I'd want to live with.

Many older people feel there shouldn't be any kind of sex life at their age. They're very moral people. They never read Masters and Johnson. Even if an older couple do not have intercourse, I'm sure they'd get pleasure from each other's bodies, from being close to each other, from lying next to each other, from handling each other.

I find myself attracted to younger men. I love the way they look. I'm a pushover for beauty. And if I were to go to bed with a man it would be with one who was younger.

I love people, and I think women are pretty wonderful. Of course I support the Equal Rights Amendment. How could I not? Women have had to bear the brunt of everything—in a marriage, in a life. I think I was liberated way before there was an organized movement.

I think my greatest strength is my buoyancy, my desire to be alive and my enjoyment of life. I'm observant. I think I'm touched by things that go on. I am never indifferent to anything. This keeps me young in spirit.

My greatest fault is that I'm sometimes overbearing in my attitude, in my beliefs, without meaning to be. Sometimes I'm dogmatic, and I'm sorry later.

I cry at great beauty whether it's in a phrase of music, something in a painting or poetry. I cry when something touches me in a play, a wonderful performance by an actor or actress. And I cry for real honest-to-goodness corn, a tear-jerker of a movie. I can weep until my handkerchief is drenched, all the time hating myself for it.

There's one last thing I'd like to say about growing older. You tell them that age doesn't necessarily make someone wise or necessarily mellow. It can, and when it does it's lovely. I think for young people to know old people is a very wonderful thing. It gives them a sense of continuity. If they're willing to listen while they're growing up, it's a way of knowing that there was something before them and there will be something after them. This to me is the value of being in the company of older people.

Hildegarde

SUPPER CLUB ENTERTAINER

Hildegarde has been in show business for over half a century. When I thought about the "First Lady of Supper Clubs," the first associations that came to mind were her trademarks: the white lace handkerchief, the long gloves and the roses.

I make my initial contact through her managers. They insist that, before meeting her, I watch her work. So on a warm, rainy evening in June I go to the Ballroom, a night spot in the part of lower Manhattan known as SoHo. Hildegarde makes her entrance from the street, sweeping in to appreciative applause, a commanding presence in chiffon and feathers.

In her act, Hildegarde frequently refers to her age: "I reverse my age, thirty-seven. And, if you add twelve, well, then I'm just forty-nine and that's not too bad." And she says as a segue: "The trend today in music is to go back to another era and since I've already been there . . ." She launches into "Thoroughly Modern Millie" and other songs of the twenties.

Her recordings of a number of songs have sold over a

million copies each: "Darling, Je Vous Aime Beaucoup" (her theme song), "I'll Be Seeing You," "The Last Time I Saw Paris," "All of a Sudden My Heart Sings" and the famed World War II song, "Lily Marlene." This evening she sings them all. The audience loves it.

A week later, we talk over four o'clock tea at the Barclay Hotel. Standing in the lobby waiting for her to appear, I wonder if she'll carry gloves, or a rose. She spots me and quickly crosses the lobby, her hand outstretched in greeting. She wears slacks and a blazer. Hildy, as she's affectionately called by her managers, smiles brightly at the people who wave to her. She converses with the headwaiter in German.

Fifty-three years in show business and still going strong, author of the book, *Over Fifty . . . So What,* Hildegarde talks about her life with animation, the upper part of her body in constant motion, her hands fluttering and gesturing in dramatic emphasis.

I was born in a little town in Wisconsin. We moved to Milwaukee when I was fourteen. I went to a Catholic high school and to Marquette University. After that I got into show business. One Saturday afternoon I went to the Palace Theater. I saw a beautiful act on stage there called "Jerry and Her Baby Grands"— four white pianos and the girl pianists dressed in colonial costumes. It was a gorgeous thing and I just fell in love with the act, wishing I could be one of the pianists. And so destiny pushed me backstage and I met the woman who was the directress. She gave me an audition, and I played "Twelfth Street Rag." Three weeks later she wired me to join their junior act.

Music was my life, even at an early age. At seven, Mother taught me piano even though I preferred to play outdoors. She had a hard time making me practice. But she'd say, "If you don't practice, you'll have to do the dishes." So I'd practice.

I always had ambitions to be in music. I played for gymnasium classes. I played for silent pictures even as a young girl. I visualized myself as a concert pianist. I had some teachers but they were second-rate until we moved to Milwaukee, where I had better teachers. Then I veered from classical to popular.

One job begot another, begot, begot. I was an accompanist for an Irish tenor. I was an accompanist for a great lady of comedy. There was Tony DeMarco, and many others. I was an accompanist only; I hadn't quite gotten to the place where I could branch out on my own as a performer.

When things don't go my way, I get pretty upset. But in life we can't expect everything to go our way, can we?

I came to New York and was a song plugger. I played songs for vaudevillians who wanted to have their songs published by Irving Berlin; I demonstrated the songs. That's how I learned to transpose and resolve to the key and things like that. Irving Berlin's manager encouraged me to sing the songs, too, instead of just playing them.

When I was there I met a comedian, Joe Laurie Junior, who became a great admirer of mine. He thought I had that "something extra." So he introduced me to someone from *Variety* magazine, and through that connection I met Gus Edwards. He was the great star-maker at that time; he discovered Eddie Cantor, Georgie Jessel and others. He had a flair for discovering talent. He said I should just use the name Hildegarde. (My full name is Hildegarde Loretta Sell.) He put me in one of his great vaudeville acts, *Stars on Parade*. I had the star lead.

When vaudeville became extinct, I really had to fend for myself. I had to perform on my own—which was terrible in the beginning. I always stayed behind the piano. I didn't have the courage to stand. And I shook in my heels. But still I managed to learn and to improve myself.

One day I was walking down Broadway, and I'll always remember this. I was wearing a beautiful sort of dusty-pink suit and a slouch hat, and people said, "There goes Garbo." I met an agent, who asked, "What are you doing now?"

I said, "Nothing at the moment."

He said, "Come and audition. I want to show you off to a man from London."

So I played and sang for this man, a cute song called "Listen to the German Band." I sang it with a thick German accent because Gus Edwards had asked me to be a little German immigrant girl in his act. I took to it very easily, you know, because I'm good at languages. Well, anyway, I did the audition for the man from London, and he liked me. He said, "I'm opening in September and I'd like to start my season with you."

But I couldn't leave. Father was dying; Father had cancer. And Mother said, "You cannot leave the country now."

So I had to forfeit this opportunity.

The man from London got me the next year—September 11, 1933. And I was a terrible flop! I was just awful. I just wasn't ready. It was terrible. He said I wasn't ready by ten years! I stayed the four weeks, though.

But something interesting happened there opening night—when Cole Porter and Gilbert Miller were in the audience and saw me flopping. Prior to that, in New York, I had met Gershwin and the president of Cartier's and all the very elegant people, and they were all behind me. These two gentlemen were at my opening and they saw how terribly I was doing. Finally they said, "Sing 'Listen to the German Band.' "

They remembered that I did that. They sort of saved my life that night.

After that I went to Paris and sang in a club there for

about a year. Then one day a big agent came from London and heard me. He wanted me to sing on the BBC once a month. It was a terrible trip because it was across the Channel, and I'd get seasick every single time. I was the first American to be on the BBC. I was also televised in London and Paris at a time when television was just an experiment. But the engagement in Paris was good because I sang in French. I learned to sing in Russian, Italian, Swedish and other languages. I was getting a feel of myself. My manager said, "Don't sing to the ceiling. Look at the people." I used to sing at the ceiling because I couldn't stand eye-to-eye contact. And then, finally, I was finding myself and I began to sing at all the elegant hotels. I have been associated with elegant hotels ever since.

When I go after a thing, I go after it, no matter how many times I've been rejected.

I came back from Europe to this country. I had a fifteen-minute radio program on NBC, where I played and sang with an orchestra. I was the highest-paid sustaining artist at that time. It was still a long struggle, my dear. It didn't happen overnight. It took me a long time. But with my European reputation I was doing better. I remember when Maurice Chevalier was in the audience at the Pierre Roof and I sang "Stormy Weather."

My opening night at the Ritz-Carlton was another stepping stone. I still lacked authority. The people were so noisy that I couldn't even hear my own music. It was terrible. Finally I got an idea. I tinkled on B flat, lightly, lightly, lightly, sitting at the piano. Then the audience became subdued. That's how I learned the trick: not to shout out but just to be quiet.

So it's been hard, but it's been gratifying. And now I

have the confidence and the strength to hold an audience in my concert work—two hours all by myself. It's a wonderful feeling.

I have to go back to tell you about the gloves. After the Ritz I went to the Versailles, which was *the* elegant place. Edith Piaf had started there. All the great French singers had started there. Someone from the Savoy-Plaza came to look me over and was impressed. So I went to the Savoy-Plaza, which was very chic and very popular.

At the Savoy-Plaza I met a designer who noticed that I used my hands and arms a great deal. I can't help it. I always talk with my hands. The designer suggested that I should wear gloves. He designed a black gown with black gloves. Later I wore white gloves, and sometimes beige.

I always took my gloves off for the finale, when I played a piano solo. But one night at the Palmer House in Chicago, I didn't have time to take them off, and I started to play with the gloves on. I got a tremendous ovation.

I thought, "I'll keep them on. Why should I take them off?" And a gimmick was born.

I'm not this old. I'm this young.

Also at this time at the Palmer House, I received gorgeous big roses, a big bouquet that filled my arms. A few roses fell down and a man picked them up.

I said, "Thank you. By the way, who are you, and what do you do? What is your name? I want to get acquainted with you."

And that was the beginning of my roses, for which I became so famous during the war. People would give the headwaiter twenty, fifty dollars just to get their name on my list, just to get a rose. Admirals and generals and privates—they all wanted a rose from me. It was so sweet. The flower people would say, "We'll furnish the roses if you'll mention our name," which I did. And so I was always associated with a rose. I have a rose named after me, called Hildegarde, from the Charles Perkins Nursery in the state of Washington.

A lot of things in my life happened accidentally—the gloves, the rose. And of course the hanky was always there because Mother said, "Now, children, you must have your nice hanky. We pin it to your waist with a little safety pin." And until this day I always have a hanky. Of course, I may use it too because I have little sinus problems. So sometimes I say, "It's not only for show, but it's also for blow."

I remember a special evening at the Statler in Washington. It was during the war, and General Wainwright had just been released from a Japanese concentration camp. He was pale, thin and gaunt. When they asked him what he wanted to do on his first night home, he said, "I'd like to see Hildegarde at the Statler." So he came. When I announced him, I gave him my whole bouquet of roses, and everyone in the audience stood up and applauded.

I asked, "General, what would you like me to sing?"

He said, "Sing 'Auld Lang Syne.' "

Well, the audience wept and applauded, and I just didn't know how to get out of that mood. It was so touching and thrilling. But I thought, "What am I going to do?" So I went into "Twelfth Street Rag" again. That corny piece of music really saved my life.

I have to psych myself up before a performance. I get terribly nervous, and knowing that certain people will be in the audience makes me even more nervous. I tell my managers not even to let me know they're there. I am still insecure, and I wonder if I can do my job again as well as I did last time. I never touch alcohol before a show—just my food for sustenance. Around seven o'clock I'll have broiled meat or fowl or fish and a big salad and a steamed vegetable. That's it for strength. I rest after dinner for about a half-hour, gather my thoughts and pray for success. Then I say, "After you, God," and go on. And it's always turned out all right.

*I think getting old is a privilege. It's sad
that people are so afraid of it.*

I feel at home performing before a live audience—except for the nerves. I love to conquer an audience. It's a great feeling of power, to dominate them. Otherwise they dominate you, and I won't allow it. It's my gift. That's why I have never been in television. I don't do movies. I want to *get* to the audience. The power—it wasn't always there because of lack of confidence, lack of experience. But through all these years I've acquired it, and I'm holding on to it. I have it now.

I'm part German, and I'm stubborn. When I go after a thing, I go after it, no matter how many times I'm rejected. Follow a star and pursue it. Don't give up. That's my advice, and I live by it.

I like being famous. It shows you've accomplished something, that your work has not been in vain. I have dedicated myself to my career. I was born with that impulse, that drive, that ambition. Even as a little girl I was a show-off. I would say, "Oh, I wonder who is watching me! I hope someone discovers me."

I've had a lot of disappointments in my life. See, I'm a dreamer. I'm a doer. I'm a worker. And when things don't go my way, I get pretty upset. But in life we can't expect everything to go our way, can we? And I always have to say, "Well, all right, God, you don't want it. I don't like it but I suppose I have to accept it." And I go into the Serenity Prayer: "Let me have the serenity to accept the things I cannot change, courage to change the things I can, and the wisdom to know the difference."

I've not accomplished what I want to as yet. I've had a lot of setbacks, a lot of rejections, and I've been dejected—yes, yes, yes! But I'm a very spiritual person, and I believe that God has a pattern, a reason for me being here. So I say, "All right, I've given up my personal happiness to make people happy. Now I want to continue to do this. See that I get this job. See that I do this and this and this." I outline it. I really do. But then I must wait and see what the outcome will be according to God's will.

I believe you can stave off aging by dieting and vitamins.

I'm not this *old*. I'm this *young*. I've always been this way. I just bubble up. It's a gift—getting away from the introvert to the extrovert. I think getting old is a privilege. It's sad that people are so afraid of it. Perhaps it's because with aging people get uglier, sicker. But it doesn't have to be this way. You should prepare for these days. I have always said I'm going to take care of myself.

Last February I sang in a nursing home in Milwaukee. A woman said, "Hey, how is it that we're both the same age, but I look older and you look younger than you did a year ago when you visited us?" How do you answer a woman like that?

Surely I'm going to age, but I'll fight it. I take very good care of myself. I don't smoke. I don't drink too much. I believe you can stave off aging by diet and vitamins. I've taken natural vitamins every day of my life since 1950. And you should watch that scale. Don't let yourself get heavy. Eat very few starches, very few sweets. Once in a while you've got to break down a bit. I walk a great deal. You can improve yourself if you just won't be lazy. It's all discipline.

I think I'm getting more admiration and more adulation as I get older. Children should be taught early in life to respect older people. They do in China.

I'm a night person. When I'm not out on the road or when I'm not out socially, I practice from nine till eleven-thirty at night. And then I do my desk work and my reading. During the day, you see, I'm busy with charity work and meeting people. I get to bed at two or three in the morning, and I try to get my eight or nine hours sleep, and by then the day is half gone. So then the night is there for me to be quiet.

I like quietness. I don't have the radio or television on. People get hypnotized by that box. I think a great deal. I plan. I concentrate on what I'm doing. I commune with God. I must be by myself to get things done. I work better.

I've been reading since I was three. I have a library of five thousand books. I read three or four books at a time: only good things, some spiritual books and a good historical novel every once in a while.

I believe that women have been liberated. If they have intelligence, brains, ambition, they should have the same respect in salary and in position as the men do. That is true. Yes, yes, yes! After all, it's the brain that matters. It's your know-how. It's your talents.

But otherwise the movement is going too far in liberating women too much. A woman still has to be feminine. Her position as mother and wife should be still respected as it used to be. I'm a traditionalist at heart. I believe that the family is very important and religion is very important. I hate that *Ms*. It sounds like a bug in heat. I can't stand that. You're either *Miss* or *Mrs*.

I'm not for abortion. That's murder. It's a sin. It's God who gives life and takes life. That's how I was taught. That's what the Catholic church teaches. That's my opinion.

There's too much permissiveness. I'm shocked at what's going on in this world. I'm not a prude; I'm not puritanical. Yet I'm shocked at the boldness, the things people do without any compunction. I wasn't raised that way. I've had many a romance, but sweet and quiet and nice. This would be a much better world if it wouldn't be all that open.

When I was growing up, everything was more decent. Television and radio weren't here. There was hardly any crime. People had a different standard of morals. I was a very obedient girl to my parents. I respected my mother and father. Now the parents are scared of their own children.

I'm shocked at the boldness, the things people do without any compunction. I've had many a romance, but they were sweet and quiet and nice.

I've always traveled a great deal, always on the road— here today, gone tomorrow. The three times I was deeply in love, I always had to leave. Subsequently these men died. I wanted to get married because I love children. Even to this day, when I see a child something tugs at my heart.

And then I think, "Well, kid, you wanted it this way." Instead of my personal happiness, I can give it to the world. I've resigned myself to it. I'm dedicated to my work, to my religion, to my friends. I'm fulfilled. I've wanted to express myself musically and I've done that.

The supper-club world has been a great schooling for me. Now I'd like to raise myself to the concert field. I'm ready to play with symphonies. Those are my new motives and ambitions. I've been in show business fifty-three years. I have three to four hundred scrapbooks. I think I have something to say. Maybe in the next few years they'll make a documentary film of me for television.

I never really thought about an epitaph for myself. I'm sort of a humble person. Nothing special: "She did her best." "She gave everything to others." Something like that. I live for others before I live for myself. It seems that's the way my life is.

Living each day spurs me on. I do my duties. I just say, "Thank you, Lord. I'll see what I can do today." Yesterday you learned something, and that's gone. Today you live. And tomorrow you plan for.

HILDEGARDE, supper club entertainer: The supper club world has been a great schooling for me. Now I'd like to raise myself to the concert field. I'm ready to play with symphonies. Those are my new motives and ambitions.

BIBLIOGRAPHY

BOOKS

BUTLER, ROBERT N. *Why Survive? Being Old in America.* New York: Harper & Row, 1975.
Comprehensive, authoritative reference work. Pulitzer Prize, 1976.

———. *Sex After Sixty: A Guide for Men and Women in Their Later Years.* New York: Harper & Row, 1976.
Active sex in later years as a reality. Honest, fact-filled.

COMFORT, ALEX. *A Good Age.* New York: Crown Publishers, 1976.
Shatters myths on aging; deals with positive realities.

CURTIN, SHARON R. *Nobody Ever Died of Old Age: In Praise of Old People . . . In Outrage at Their Loneliness.* Boston: Little, Brown, 1972.
A nurse's firsthand reaction to how we treat the elderly.

FARBER, NORMA. *How Does It Feel to Be Old?* Illustrated by Trina Schart Hyman. New York: E. P. Dutton, 1979.
Children's book about relationship between a lonely old woman and a child. Beautifully executed.

GLIMCHER, ARNOLD. *Louise Nevelson.* New York: Dutton, 1976.
Biography of a nonconformist sculptor, still active in her seventies. Photographs.

GORDON, RUTH. *My Side.* New York: Harper & Row, 1976.
Autobiography of an actress, written on the eve of her eightieth birthday. Strong and vibrant. Photographs.

GROSS, RONALD; GROSS, BEATRICE; SEIDMAN, SYLVIA. *The New Old: Struggling for Decent Aging.* New York: Anchor Press, Doubleday, 1978.
Compilation of articles. Thorough, thought-provoking.

KANIN, GARSON. *It Takes a Long Time to Become Young.* New York: Doubleday, 1978.
Hard-hitting, lively indictment of mandatory retirement.

KNOPF, OLGA. *Successful Aging.* New York: Viking Press, 1975. Written by an eighty-seven-year-old psychiatrist. Practical advice.

KUHN, MAGGIE. *On Aging: A Dialogue.* Edited by Dieter Hessel. Philadelphia: Westminster Press, 1977. Question-and-answer format. Action guide on aging; outspoken and down-to-earth.

MYERHOFF, BARBARA. *Number Our Days.* New York: E. P. Dutton, 1978. An anthropologist's in-depth study of a Jewish community in California. Absorbing sense of history.

NUDEL, ADELE. *For the Woman Over 50: A Practical Guide for a Full and Vital Life.* New York: Taplinger, 1978. Comprehensive, practical advice. Easy to read.

TROLL, LILLIAN E.; ISRAEL, JOAN; ISRAEL, KENNETH. *Looking Ahead: A Woman's Guide to the Problems and Joys of Growing Older.* Englewood Cliffs, N. J.: Prentice-Hall, 1977. Compilation of articles on a wide variety of topics for women approaching midlife and later years. Thorough reference list at end of each chapter.

MAGAZINES AND PAMPHLETS

AGING
Administration on Aging, Room 4551
330 Independence Avenue, S.W.
Washington, D.C. 20201
Official magazine of National Clearinghouse on Aging. Describes federal regulations, new government programs.

OPTIONS
News for Older New Yorkers
New York City Department for the Aging
250 Broadway
New York, N.Y. 10007
Newspaper format. Programs, profiles, book reviews, money-saving tips.

50 PLUS
850 Third Avenue
New York, N.Y. 10022
  Glossy monthly magazine.
Variety of information, wide appeal.

IMAGES OF OLD AGE IN THE AMERICAN MEDIA
American Jewish Committee
165 East 56th Street
New York, N.Y. 10022
  Conference report, 1978.

MODERN MATURITY
American Association of Retired Persons
1909 K Street, N.W.
Washington, D.C. 20049
  Bimonthly. General information and
advice for older adults.

THE AGING IN AMERICA
Implications for Women by Tish Sommers (1976)
National Council on the Aging
1828 L Street, N.W.
Washington, D.C. 20036
  Based on Louis Harris & Associates
public-opinion study, "The Myth
and Reality of Aging in America."

SENIOR SUMMARY
New York Junior League
130 East 80th Street
New York, N.Y. 10021
  Quarterly, large-print newspaper. News,
activities, events for older adults.

SEXUAL LIFE IN THE LATER YEARS
Siecus Publications Office
1855 Broadway
New York, N.Y. 10023
  Study guide recognizing the normality of
sexuality and sexual expression in later years.

RESOURCE GROUPS AND ORGANIZATIONS

Administration on Aging
Office of Human Development
330 Independence Avenue, S.W.
Washington, D.C. 20201

American Association of Retired Persons (AARP)
1909 K Street, N.W.
Washington, D.C. 20036

Gray Panthers
6342 Greene Street
Philadelphia, Pa. 19144

International Senior Citizens Association
11753 Wilshire Boulevard
Los Angeles, Calif. 90025

National Action Forum for Older Women
Health Sciences Center
State University of New York
Stony Brook, N.Y. 11794

National Caucus on the Black Aged
1730 M Street, N.W.
Washington, D.C. 20036

National Council on the Aging
1828 L Street, N.W.
Washington, D.C. 20036

National Senior Citizens Law Center
1200 15th Street, N.W.
Washington, D.C. 20005

Older Women's League
3800 Harrison Street
Oakland, Calif. 94611

Pension Rights Center
1346 Connecticut Avenue, N.W.
Washington, D.C. 20036

For information about the Foster Grandparent Program, check with local department for the aging.

Afterthought

To be nobody but yourself, in a world which is doing its best night and day to make you just like anyone else, means to fight the greatest battle there is to fight and never stop fighting.

e. e. cummings